get hooked again

Simple Steps to Crochet MORE Cool Stuff

by Kim Werker

Photography by Angela Fama
and Pamela Bethel
Illustrations by Cynthia Frenette

WATSON-GUPTILL PUBLICATIONS / NEW YORK

Senior Acquisitions Editor: Julie Mazur
Editor: Linda Hetzer
Designer: Margo Mooney
Production Manager: Alyn Evans

First published in 2007 by Watson-Guptill Publications,
Nielsen Business Media, a division of The Nielsen Company
770 Broadway, New York, NY 10003
www.watsonguptill.com

Library of Congress Control Number: 2007920865

ISBN-10: 0-8230-5110-2
ISBN-13: 0-978-8230-5110-6

Printed in China

First printing, 2007

1 2 3 4 5 6 7 8 / 14 13 12 11 10 09 08 07

Dedication

To Mom and Dad. Thanks for supporting me in all my crazy adventures, and even when I decided not to get my PhD. I love you.

Acknowledgments

Big, huge thanks to all the designers who made the awesome patterns in this book. I had so much fun working with them and can't wait to see the great stuff they make in the future. Julie Holetz also technical edited all of the patterns to make sure they are as clear and accurate as possible, and she totally rocks.

To my editors, Julie Mazur and Linda Hetzer, thank you for your patience and creativity, and for being so much fun to work with. I will jump at any chance I have to work with Cynthia Frenette, Angela Fama, and Pam Bethel again. Warm They are three of the most talented visual artists I know. thanks go to the yarn companies that generously supplied the materials used to make the projects.

Hugs to the Werkers and Feldmans for loving me and for being excited about crochet because I love it, to the Fiber League for advice and friendship, and to Scott and Carol for making home feel more like home. Biggest thanks of all to Greg, for knowing me so well, for feeding me yummy food, and for wearing that cuddly brown sweater.

Contents

Introduction

GET YOUR CROCHET ON

Crochet is the wildly fun activity of interlocking loops of yarn with a crochet hook. Okay. That sounded SO uncool. But it really is cool and fun and so simple! You can make anything—hats, scarves, mitts, jewelry, leg warmers, sweaters, vests, blankets, toys. If you can imagine it, you can crochet it. Cool, huh?

Once you've mastered the simple basics of crochet, you can make all sorts of things to express your personal style—and to give as gifts to your friends and family. All you need is yarn and a hook! Crochet is portable, so you can work on your project while you ride the bus, wait for a doctor's appointment, watch TV, or even hang out with your friends. Hey, that's an idea. . . . Learn to crochet with your friends and you can give one another a constant supply of fun presents.

So, let's review: Crochet is easy. It's fun. It's cool. Are you hooked yet?

Tricks of the Trade

Here are some things to keep in mind as you get started crocheting:

* Take a deep breath and follow the instructions, one step at a time. Don't expect to be an expert immediately!

* If something baffles you, take a break. Walk the dog or read a chapter in your current novel, then come back to it.

* Beginning crocheters usually crochet pretty tightly. This is normal! As you get used to the motions of crochet, you'll relax—and so will your stitches.

* Since you might crochet tightly in the beginning, make sure you take frequent breaks so your fingers and wrists don't get sore. If you do experience any pain, put down your project and tell an adult right away.

Stocking Up

You don't need many supplies to dive into crocheting. But take a minute to learn about the tools and materials you do need—and get them before you start your first project so you can avoid last-minute trips to the crafts store!

Get Hooked

A **crochet hook** is really the only tool you need to get started. Hooks come in many varieties, but the basics are always the same. They're usually made of plastic, aluminum, bamboo, or wood; and the tiniest hooks (used to crochet thin threads) are made of steel.

Experiment with different kinds of hooks so you can find the ones you're most comfortable with. You might even find that you prefer using one type of hook with a particular kind of yarn—such as plastic hooks with wool yarn or wooden hooks with acrylic.

THE ANATOMY OF A HOOK

Two factors determine what kind of hook is appropriate for a particular yarn: the depth of the hook and the width of its shaft.

The **depth** of the hook affects how easily you can grab the yarn with it, which mostly ends up being a matter of personal preference. That's why you should experiment with hooks from different manufacturers until you find the ones you like the best!

The **width** of the hook's shaft determines the size of the hook. The wider the diameter of the shaft, the larger your stitches will be and the heavier weight yarn you can use comfortably with the hook. The narrower the shaft, the smaller your stitches will be and the finer the yarn you can use.

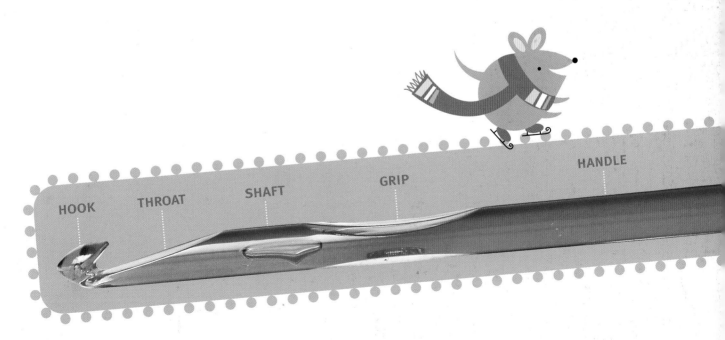

HOOK   THROAT   SHAFT   GRIP   HANDLE

HOOK SIZE

Hooks come in all sizes! Unfortunately, there isn't a universal standard in North America for how to label these sizes, so you'll often see two sizes given for the same hook: the metric size and the American size.

The metric size is based on the actual metric measurement of the diameter of the hook's shaft, given in millimeters (mm). In the American system, sizes of most hooks are given in letters, and the tiny steel hook sizes are given in numbers (but the numbers don't correspond to an actual measurement!). The American system is pretty arbitrary, and there isn't always a direct relationship between the American size and the metric size. Different hook brands might even give the same metric-sized hook a different letter size! It's confusing, but this chart can help you. For each project in this book, the recommended hook size is listed in metric first, followed by the American size in parentheses—for example: 5.0mm (size H) crochet hook.

The tiny steel hooks, which are used for fine threads, range in size from 0.75mm (size 14) to 3.5mm (size 00). They're usually used with cotton crochet threads of all weights and with fingering weight yarns. Non-steel hooks range in size from 2.25mm (size B)—yup, these sizes overlap with steel hook sizes!—to 19.0mm (size S) or even larger.

Hook Sizes

METRIC SIZE	AMERICAN SIZE	STEEL HOOK SIZE
0.75mm		14
0.85mm		13
1.0mm		12
1.1mm		11
1.3mm		10
1.4mm		9
1.5mm		8
1.65mm		7
1.8mm		6
1.9mm		5
2.0mm		4
2.1mm		3
2.25mm	B	2
2.75mm	C	1
3.25mm	D	0
3.5mm	E	00
3.75mm	F	
4.0mm	G	
4.5mm		
5.0mm	H	
5.5mm	I	
6.0mm	J	
6.5mm	K	
7.0mm		
8.0mm	L	
9.0mm	M/N	
10.0mm	N/P	
15.0mm	P/Q	
16.0mm	Q	
19.0mm	S	

Leftie or Rightie?

You'll probably be most comfortable holding your hook in the same hand you use for writing, but try using your other hand just to see how it feels. Remember, too, that your hook hand isn't the only important hand when you crochet. Your other hand holds the fabric as you create it and keeps the tension of the yarn regular as it feeds it to your hook so your stitches come out even. Righties and lefties crochet in opposite directions—but both ways are correct!

From the Heart

Crocheting for charity is a great thing to do! There are dozens upon dozens of local and national organizations that will gladly accept handmade goods to distribute to people who need them.

What works Lots of patterns in this book would make perfect items to donate. Scarves keep everyone warm—and stylish looking! Hats are super valuable not only for battling a cold winter, but also for people who are ill. Make these caps out of the softest yarn you can find, since people who are sick are often very sensitive. Slippers may also be welcome at shelters and hospitals. Just make sure you ask first if slippers with slippery soles are acceptable.

Use your imagination If you know of a local organization you'd like to support, call to find out what is needed. Or see page 94 for help finding a list of charities online.

Enlist your posse Don't go it alone. Crocheting for charity is more fun when you do it with friends. You can have your friends make two items: one to donate and one to give to another friend as a gift or to use themselves. (Um, who said you shouldn't want to keep some of the goodies for yourself?)

Yarn, Yarn, Yarn

If your crochet hook is like the straw for your Slurpy, then yarn is the icy goodness. It comes in so many colors, textures, and weights, you could spend a lifetime trying out new ones. Here's an overview of what to look for in yarn.

FIBER Every yarn is composed of fibers, which can be generally categorized as natural or synthetic. **Natural** fibers come from animals (such as sheep, camels, alpacas, rabbits, and silkworms) or plants (such as cotton, hemp, soy, and bamboo). **Synthetic** fibers are made from chemicals, and include acrylic, nylon, and polyester. You can find both affordable and expensive yarns of each type; but as a general rule, the most expensive yarns are made from rare natural fibers and the least expensive yarns are often synthetics. Natural fibers tend to be warm and breathable, and they usually require gentle hand washing. Synthetic fibers come in a huge assortment of colors and textures and can often be machine washed. Many yarns contain a blend of natural and synthetic fibers, so they benefit from the qualities of both. Every yarn is labeled with its fiber content (see page 15).

CONSTRUCTION Yarn can also be categorized according to two general types of construction: traditional and novelty. **Traditional** yarns are usually smooth looking. Sometimes they are also *plied,* which means that two or more thinner strands of yarn are twisted together to make a thicker, stronger strand. **Novelty** yarns have funky textures such as fun fur, bouclé, and ribbon; and they sometimes have bits and pieces of other materials spun into the yarn. As a beginner, it's a good idea to stick with traditional yarns for your first few projects. These yarns show off stitches very clearly, which will help you count the stitches as your work progresses and also see any mistakes you may have made. Once you're comfortable with the basics, you can play with nifty novelty yarns all you want!

WEIGHT The last major way to categorize yarns is by their weight—not by how much they actually weigh on a scale, but by how thin or thick the yarn is.

Yarn weight ranges from **super fine** to **super bulky.** The thinner the yarn, the smaller the hook you use; the bulkier the yarn, the larger the hook. We've included a chart from the Craft Yarn Council of America (at the right) so you can see how yarn companies categorize the weight of their yarns.

Although most patterns specify a particular yarn to use, you can easily substitute a different one that is the same weight and that you crochet to the same gauge listed in the pattern (see page 33 for more on gauge).

The Craft Yarn Council of America's Standard Yarn Weight System

YARN WEIGHT CATEGORY	SYMBOL	TYPES OF YARN	HOW MANY SINGLE CROCHET STITCHES IN 4 INCHS?	RECOMMENDED HOOK SIZES (U.S.)	RECOMMENDED HOOK SIZES (METRIC)
Super fine	1 SUPER FINE	Sock, fingering, baby	21–32 stitches	B to E	2.25–3.5 mm
Fine	2 FINE	Sport, baby	16–20 stitches	E to G	3.5–4.5 mm
Light	3 LIGHT	DK, light worsted	12–17 stitches	G to I	4.5–5.5 mm
Medium	4 MEDIUM	Worsted, afghan, aran	11–14 stitches	I to K	5.5–6.5 mm
Bulky	5 BULKY	Chunky, craft, rug	8–11 stitches	K to M	6.5–9 mm
Super bulky	6 SUPER BULKY	Bulky, roving	5–9 stitches	M and larger	9mm and larger

This table shows the six major yarn weight categories. If you like a pattern but want to use a different yarn, make sure you choose one that's in the same weight category as the one specified in the pattern.

It Felt Smaller . . .

Wool yarns might **felt** when they're agitated in the wash. This means that the fibers bind together to form a thick, durable fabric that's smaller in size than the unfelted version. If you've ever shrunk a wool sweater in the wash, this is what happened! Some wool yarns have been chemically treated so that they won't felt; these are called **superwash,** and you can machine wash items you make from this kind of yarn.

BUYING YARN

Yarn comes packaged in one of three ways.

A **ball** is somewhat spherical. You use the yarn by unraveling it from the outside of the ball.

A **skein** is more of a cylinder. You use the yarn either by unraveling it from the outside or by fishing around in the center of the skein to find the other end. It's usually easier to pull the yarn from the center of a skein, so pull out the end and use the yarn from there.

A **hank** is a loosely wound ring of yarn, often sold twisted into a shape you might mistake for a skein. A hank needs to be rewound into a ball or a skein before you use the yarn. Otherwise, it will tangle into an unusable mess.

Using a center-pull skein is easy, since the skein can rest on the couch next to you and not move as you pull the yarn from it. If you're using a ball of yarn, or if you have pets, put the ball into a zipper-lock plastic bag. Pull the end of the yarn out of the bag, then zip the bag most of the way closed. This secures the ball and keeps it away from pets.

So, where can you find great yarn to buy? Yarn is sold in local yarn stores that specialize in selling yarns and tools for knitters and crocheters. You can also find yarn in large crafts centers and sometimes in big-box stores. There are also tons of online yarn stores, and lots of people sell yarn on eBay too.

Shown here:
a hank (blue),
a skein (green),
and a ball
(purple).

Don't Rewind Me

Here's the best (and most fun) way to wind a hank of yarn into a ball.

1. Have your winding partner untwist the hank and wrap it around her forearms. You are going to unwrap the yarn from her arms and wind it into a ball.

2. Start by winding the yarn several times around your first two fingers.

3. Then remove the yarn from your fingers and continue to wind the yarn around itself, changing directions every so often so you end up with a ball.

If you're stuck winding a ball of yarn by yourself, try sitting on the floor with the hank wrapped around your feet or knees, or putting the hank around the back of a chair or even around your neck.

HOW TO READ A YARN LABEL

Yarn comes with a label that tells you every-thing you need to know about it.

QUANTITY The weight (in ounces and/or grams) and length (in yards and/or meters) of the skein is given on the label. This information is very important for helping you figure out how many balls, skeins, or hanks of yarn you'll need to buy, especially if you're substituting the yarn called for in the pattern (you'll need to make sure you have the same length called for if you're using yarn of the same weight!).

FIBER CONTENT The label tells you what kind(s) of fibers make up the yarn, and in what proportion.

DYE LOT Yarn doesn't start out in pretty colors—it's often dyed! Since only a limited quantity of yarn can be dyed at any one time, slight variations may occur between batches. Each batch is given a *dye lot* number so you can be sure that the yarn you are buying was all dyed in the same batch.

RECOMMENDED HOOK SIZE Since each person crochets differently—more loosely or tightly—remember that the hook size given on a yarn label is only a suggestion. If the label only recommends a knitting needle size, use a crochet hook of the same metric size as the needle or one size larger. Really, the most important factor in choosing a hook size is your ability to crochet to the gauge specified in the pattern you choose (more on gauge on page 33)!

CARE INSTRUCTIONS The label specifies, usually in symbols, how to wash and dry items made from the yarn. For example, the symbols on the label pictured indicate, from left to right, that items should be washed by hand, should not be bleached, and should be dried flat. Don't ignore these specifications! After you've spent lots of time and possibly lots of money on your crochet project, make sure you do everything you can to take care of it.

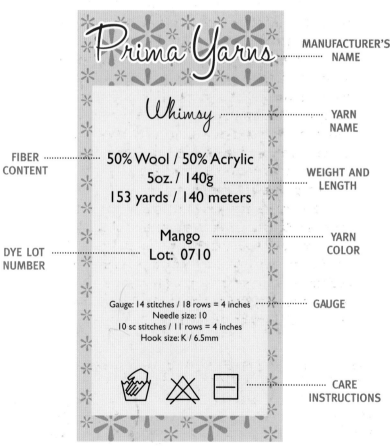

FIBER CONTENT

DYE LOT NUMBER

Prima Yarns

MANUFACTURER'S NAME

Whimsy

YARN NAME

50% Wool / 50% Acrylic
5oz. / 140g
153 yards / 140 meters

WEIGHT AND LENGTH

Mango
Lot: 0710

YARN COLOR

Gauge: 14 stitches / 18 rows = 4 inches
Needle size: 10
10 sc stitches / 11 rows = 4 inches
Hook size: K / 6.5mm

GAUGE

CARE INSTRUCTIONS

DECISIONS, DECISIONS

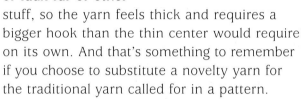

You might prefer to follow a pattern to the letter, especially if you're new to yarn and hooks. Or you may be an adventurous crocheter, making up your project as you go. Either way, there's a lot to think about when you embark upon a new project!

If you like to follow patterns, how do you choose? There are so many! First, look for one that catches your eye. Maybe it's a pattern you've never seen before and you think it'll be fun to experiment. Maybe it's an item you've seen in all the stores but want to make yourself. It doesn't matter why it's appealing, just go with it!

Next comes a decision about what yarn to use. First, what texture? All of the patterns in this book use smooth yarns of traditional construction. But if the yarn specified doesn't appeal to you, or it's too expensive, or you can't find it, simply substitute another yarn that's the same weight as the one called for (see page 13 for more on yarn weights). And if you're comfortable with your crochet skills, you can totally experiment with funky yarns even though they'll make your stitches—and

mistakes—harder to see. Keep in mind that although many textured novelty yarns have fairly thin centers, they're usually covered with fuzz or faux fur or other stuff, so the yarn feels thick and requires a bigger hook than the thin center would require on its own. And that's something to remember if you choose to substitute a novelty yarn for the traditional yarn called for in a pattern.

And finally, what color to use? Lots of people use the exact same yarn in the exact same color that's shown in the pattern. I've always wondered why they do this—there's so much room to be creative! Go with your mood, your favorite color, the season . . . the possibilities are endless. And as you'll learn on the following pages, adding a bunch of different colors to your crochet is super easy. So even if a pattern is shown in one color, you can easily add stripes! It's just one more way you can be creative with your crochet.

Nifty Notions

Okay, so you do need a few more things besides a hook and yarn. Having a few tools handy will enable you to work on your projects neatly and with fewer interruptions. These items can be found in almost any crafts or yarn store.

A **yarn needle** (sometimes called a tapestry needle) is bigger than a sewing needle, has a blunt tip, and has a bigger eye to accommodate thicker yarns. Use a yarn needle to weave in yarn ends when you've finished a project and to sew seams when it comes time to assemble it.

A **tape measure** is used to—*duh*—take measurements! Measure your head or chest circumference so you can figure out which size hat or top to make. Measure your gauge (see page 33). Measure your cat!

Stitch markers allow you to mark a specific place in your project. Some patterns call for you to mark a stitch so you know when a round begins or ends (see page 36 for more on working in the round). Others call for you to mark a stitch for later reference—maybe that's a place where you'll fold the piece to seam it or where you'll join yarn later. Crochet stitch markers are placed directly into a stitch, so you have to be able to open and close them. Avoid using safety pins that have a coil, because the yarn can get stuck in the coil and break or shred.

A **row counter** is a handy tool to help you keep track of how many rows you've crocheted. You can also keep track by making a pencil mark on your pattern for every completed row.

It's also a good idea to keep scissors handy, and maybe even a calculator, if you want to adjust a pattern size.

Tip

For stitch markers, try an earring! Just make sure to use one that opens and closes, so it will stay put in your work.

Clockwise from top: Scissors, tape measure, row counter, yarn needles, stitch markers, wheel of straight pins.

The Language of Patterns

Think of crochet patterns as recipes or as directions for how to get to your friend's house. They may look intimidating at first, but if you just follow them one step at a time, you'll be fine!

The very beginning of a pattern lists information about all the things you'll need—yarn, hook size, notions, and any special materials such as buttons, sewing thread, or glue. There's also information about the size of the finished project (that's especially important if you're making a garment or a hat) and also about the gauge you need to crochet to in order for your project to end up the right size (more about gauge on page 33).

Next comes the pattern itself. Read through the whole thing once or twice so you get a good idea of what you'll be doing. Take a good look at the schematic drawings, too, to understand how the project is constructed. Also, be sure to check out the directions for how to finish the project and study any special stitch patterns that are used—you can practice these when you make your gauge swatch (see page 33).

Crochet patterns are generally written as a set of row-by-row (when you're making rectangles) or round-by-round (when you're making circles or ovals) instructions. Every publication—whether it's a magazine or a book or a website—has its own style of pattern writing, but the approach is the same.

If there is a group of stitches that is repeated several times in one row or round, it will be placed between **asterisks** (* *) and referred to as "Repeat from * to * X number of times." For example, "*Single crochet in each of the next 2 stitches, double crochet in the next stitch*, repeat from * to * to the end of the row" means that you should single crochet in each of the next two stitches, then double crochet in the next stitch, over and over until you get to the end of the row.

A Substitute for Today

Sometimes you might want to use a different yarn from the one listed in the pattern. No problem! Just be sure to pick a yarn that's the same weight (see the chart on page 13 for more on yarn weights) and that's made up of the same type of fibers. The fiber content is important, because different types of fibers behave differently once they're stitched up, and you'll want to make sure you get a finished project that's like the one pictured in the pattern. To help you get started, in each of the patterns in the book we've listed what type of yarn you can substitute for the yarn used in the project.

Brackets (straight or curvy) and **parentheses** are also used to help make the pattern easier to understand. Sometimes several stitches are worked into the same stitch from the previous row or round. In that case, you'll see instructions such as "Work [double crochet, chain 1, double crochet] into the next stitch," which means you should make all three stitches in the same stitch from the previous row or round.

If a pattern calls for more than one color of yarn, the colors are indicated as **Color A, Color B, Color C,** and so on. This makes it easy if you want to use different colors from the ones indicated in the pattern.

The patterns in this book are written out in full sentences, but most crochet patterns are written in crochet shorthand using lots of abbreviations (such as **sc** for **single crochet**). This is because crochet instructions can get pretty long, and using shorthand makes the patterns as short and concise as possible. When you need some help making sense of abbreviations, use this chart, which lists the most common ones, and you'll have no trouble keeping up.

Abbreviations

ABBREVIATION	TRANSLATION
approx	**approximately**
beg	begin/beginning
bet	**between**
blo or BLO	back loop only
CC	**contrasting color**
ch(s) or CH(S)	chain(s)
ch sp or CH-SP or ch-sp	**chain space**
cont	continue/continuing
dc or DC	**double crochet**
dec or DEC	decrease/decreasing
flo or FLO	**front loop only**
hdc or HDC	half double crochet
hk or HK	**hook**
inc or INC	increase/increasing
lp(s) or LP(S)	**loop(s)**
MC	main color
pat or patt	**pattern**
pm or PM	place marker
prev	**previous**
rem	remain/remaining
rnd(s) or RND(S)	**round(s)**
sc or SC	single crochet
sl st or Sl St or SS	**slip stitch**
st(s) or ST(S)	stitch(es)
tog or TOG	**together**
tr or TR	treble (triple) crochet
yo or YO	**yarn over**

Getting Started

Time to put your fingers to work! This chapter will tell you everything you need to get started, from how to hold your hook to how to make all the basic stitches.

Crochet 101

Crochet is what happens when you use a hook to connect loops of yarn. It's as simple as that!

You start by making several **chains** that are connected to each other. This makes up a **foundation chain** that serves as—you guessed it—the foundation for your whole project. Once you've made the foundation chain, you work the first row of crochet stitches into its loops and then you make row after row of stitches on top of each other. The pattern you choose will tell you exactly what to do.

There's a huge variety of stitches you can use in crochet, and each results in a different-looking fabric. This book will teach you the basic stitches, but there are many books and websites that can show you how to make lots more. The cool part is that pretty much all of those other stitch patterns use these basic stitches, so once you master these, there's no limit to what you can create!

All the Right Moves

Getting comfortable with crochet means getting comfortable with three basic moves that are done in a continuous motion—inserting the hook into a space or stitch, wrapping the yarn around the hook (called a **yarn over**), and then pulling the yarn through the loop.

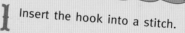

1 Insert the hook into a stitch.

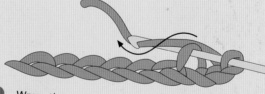

2 Wrap the yarn around the hook from back to front. This is called a yarn over.

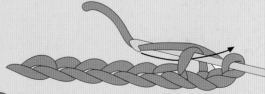

3 Grab the yarn with the hook and draw it through the stitch.

First Things First

Don't just stare at that hook and yarn! Here's what to do with them.

GET A GRIP

There are basically two ways you can hold your hook—like a knife or like a pencil. Try them both to see which one you like better.

Like a knife

Like a pencil

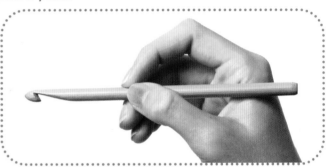

START WITH A SLIP KNOT

The first step is to secure your yarn to your hook so you can start crocheting. You do this with a **slip knot.**

1 Hold the long end of the yarn in one hand, about 8 inches from the end. With your other hand, loop the end of the yarn behind the yarn you're holding.

2 Pull some of the long end of the yarn through the loop and grab it with your hook.

3 Pull up your hook while holding the yarn below it. Tug on each strand of yarn to tighten the loop on your hook. Don't make the loop too tight—it should be snug, but loose enough to slide freely along the shaft.

In Stitches

Okay, so you've attached the yarn to your hook. What's next? Here's how to make the basic crochet stitches.

CHAIN STITCH

The **chain stitch** (abbreviated as **ch**) is the basis of all crochet, and it couldn't be easier: you draw one loop of yarn through another. (To make your first chain, always start with a slip knot on your hook!)

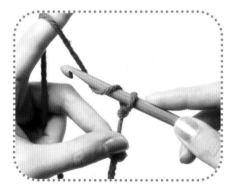  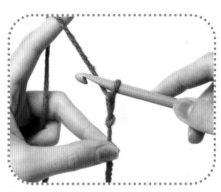

1 Wrap the yarn around your hook from back to front to back again. This is also called making a **yarn over**. Whenever you see an instruction to do a yarn over, that's what you do.

2 Grab the yarn with your hook, and draw it through the loop already on your hook.

3 You've made one chain stitch. Repeat steps 1 and 2 to make more chain stitches.

A Chain for the Better

It may seem a bit confusing that the word "chain" is used to refer to a couple different things. So let's take a minute to talk about these terms. A **chain stitch** is the most basic crochet stitch, and is the template on which all the other stitches are built.

When chain stitches are worked together in a row, this is called a **foundation chain**. When you start a project that's crocheted in rows, you will start with a foundation chain. When you start a project worked in rounds, you will work the first round into one chain stitch or into a small circle made up of a row of chain stitches attached to itself end to end.

Chain stitches are used in some patterns to create space between stitches for a lacy, open look. Chain stitches can also be used in the middle of the row to create a buttonhole. At the end or the beginning of a row, you make a **turning chain**.

SLIP STITCH

After the chain, the **slip stitch** (abbreviated as **sl st**) is the simplest crochet stitch. You won't use it to create an entire project, but it comes in handy, as you'll see!

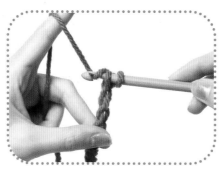

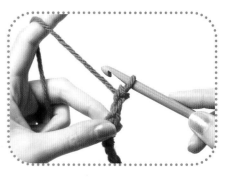

1 Insert your hook in a stitch (your pattern will tell you which one).

2 Yarn over. Then pull the yarn through both the stitch and the loop on your hook.

3 Now you have one loop on your hook, and you've completed one slip stitch. Repeat steps 1 and 2 to make your next stitch.

The Anatomy of a Chain

After you've made several chain stitches, they form a **chain.** The front side of the chain looks like a braid or a bunch of hearts made up of V's. The back of the chain looks kind of like a bumpy spine, with a ridge down the middle. Each chain stitch is made of three loops: the two loops of the V on the front side and the bump on the back.

Usually it doesn't matter which loop or loops of the chain you insert your hook into when you make your first row of stitches, but sometimes a pattern will specify to work into the *front loop*, into the *back loop*, or into the *bump on the back of the chain*.

Take care to make your chain pretty loose since you'll have to insert your hook into it later. If your chain is too tight, it will be difficult to work with and it might make the bottom edge of your work look wonky. Practice making chains until you're comfortable with the steps and the chains come out even and not too tight.

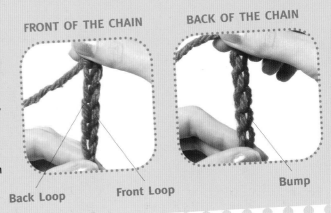

FRONT OF THE CHAIN

BACK OF THE CHAIN

Back Loop   Front Loop

Bump

SINGLE CROCHET

This next stitch, the **single crochet** (abbreviated as **sc**), is the basis for all the other crochet stitches.

This is what several rows of single crochet stitches look like.

1 Insert your hook in the next stitch.

2 Yarn over.

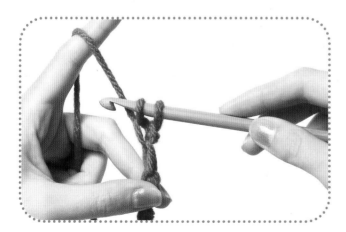

3 Grab the yarn that's over the hook and pull it through only the stitch (this is referred to as **pulling up a loop**). Now you have two loops on your hook.

4 Yarn over and pull the yarn through *both* of the loops on your hook. Now you have one loop on your hook, and you've just completed a single crochet stitch! Repeat steps 1–4 to make your next stitch.

HALF DOUBLE CROCHET

Every other crochet stitch is simply a variation of the single crochet stitch. This one is a **half double crochet** (abbreviated as **hdc**).

1 Start with a yarn over. Then insert your hook in the next stitch.

2 Yarn over and pull up a loop. You now have three loops on your hook.

3 Yarn over and pull the yarn through all three loops on your hook. Now you have one loop on your hook, and you've completed one half double crochet stitch. Repeat steps 1–3 to make your next stitch.

Tip Have you found one stitch you like the most? Lots of crocheters have a favorite, and mine is the half double crochet. There's just something about it that makes me smile—and I feel as if I crochet so fast when I make it!

DOUBLE CROCHET

As you'll notice, the stitches keep getting taller as we go. Here's a **double crochet** (abbreviated as **dc**).

1 Start with a yarn over. Then insert your hook in the next stitch.

2 Yarn over and pull up a loop. You now have three loops on your hook.

3 Yarn over and pull the yarn through the first two loops on your hook. Two loops remain on your hook.

4 Yarn over and pull the yarn through the remaining two loops on your hook. Now you have one loop on your hook, and you've completed one double crochet stitch. Repeat steps 1–4 to make your next stitch.

TREBLE CROCHET

Ready for a crazy one? This is the **treble crochet,** also called the **triple crochet** (abbreviated as **tr**). Notice how you yarn over twice at the beginning of the stitch.

1 **Yarn over twice.** This means you wrap the yarn *twice* around the hook. Then insert your hook in the next stitch.

2 Yarn over and pull up a loop. You now have four loops on your hook.

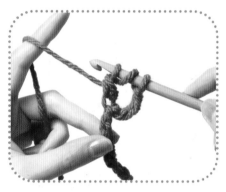

3 Yarn over and pull the yarn through the first two loops on your hook. Now you have three loops on your hook.

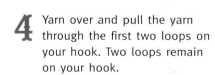

4 Yarn over and pull the yarn through the first two loops on your hook. Two loops remain on your hook.

5 Yarn over and pull the yarn through the remaining two loops on your hook. Now you have one loop on your hook, and you've completed a treble crochet stitch. Repeat steps 1–5 to make your next stitch.

She Goes in Rows

Lots of crochet projects are made by working row after row of stitches, one on top of another. Things such as scarves, bags, and many sweaters are worked in this manner. When you get to the end of a row, you turn the piece around—really, you just flip it around so the other side is facing you. Then you insert your hook into the tops of the stitches you just made to work the next row.

WHERE DO YOU PUT YOUR HOOK?

So, hmm, all this talk about making rows of stitches on top of each other. . . . How does that work exactly?

Take a look at the top of your first row of stitches (the row you made by sticking your hook into each chain of the foundation chain). You'll see that the top of a stitch looks like the front side of a chain stitch, composed of that familiar V. In most cases you insert your hook under both loops of the V. Sometimes, though, a pattern will instruct you to work through only one of the loops: the front loop only or the back loop only. Still looking at the tops of those stitches? The loop of the V that is closest to you is the **front loop,** and the loop of the V that is farthest from you is the **back loop.**

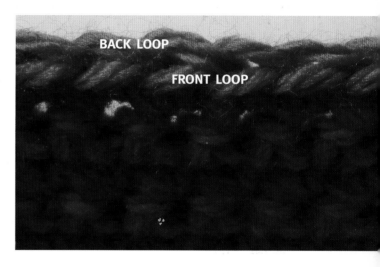

BACK LOOP

FRONT LOOP

To work into a stitch in the row below, insert your hook under both loops of the stitch.

To work into the **front loop only,** insert your hook into the loop closest to you, and work your stitches as usual.

To work into the **back loop only,** insert your hook into the loop farthest from you, and work your stitches as usual.

TURNING CHAINS

As you may have noticed from the description of stitches in the last few pages, crochet stitches can be pretty tall. When you start a new row of stitches, you need to gain the height needed to meet the top of the stitches you'll be making. If you don't, the edges of your work will get warped. You use **turning chains** to do this.

Depending on what the pattern specifies, turning chains are sometimes counted as a full stitch (this is common with the taller stitches) and sometimes they aren't. If it's important, the pattern will tell you.

Most of the time, it doesn't matter whether you make the turning chain before or after you turn your work. The pattern you use will specify when to make the turning chain.

The number of turning chains you need to make is determined by which stitch you'll be making in the next row.

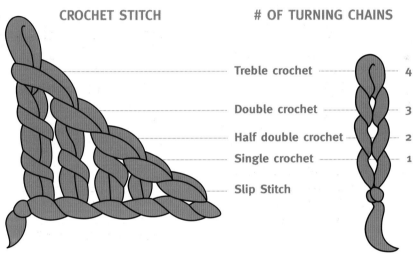

CROCHET STITCH   **# OF TURNING CHAINS**

Treble crochet	4
Double crochet	3
Half double crochet	2
Single crochet	1
Slip Stitch	

COUNTING STITCHES

You should count your stitches every few rows to make sure you have the correct number, especially when you're learning how to crochet. It's easy to miss a stitch or to accidentally work more stitches than required.

Look at your stitches from above and you'll see the familiar braid. To count your stitches, you just count the V's in the braid.

To count the stitches several rows down, you count the "posts" of the stitches. (Remember to check your pattern to see if you should count the turning chain as a stitch.)

Getting Attached

Unless you're making something very small, you'll have to use more than one skein of yarn to complete a project. When one skein runs out, you just start crocheting with another. Use this same technique to change to yarn of a different color if you're making stripes. (In these photographs, the new yarn is shown in a different color to make the steps easier to see.)

AT THE BEGINNING OF A ROW

1 Leave a tail of the old yarn dangling. Attach the new yarn to your hook with a slip knot. Then insert your hook in the first stitch of the row.

2 Yarn over with the new yarn and draw up a loop, then continue to pull the yarn through the loop on your hook to complete the slip stitch.

3 The new yarn is now attached. Continue by working the next stitch as called for in your pattern in the same place you attached the yarn.

IN THE MIDDLE OF A ROW

1 With the old yarn, work the next stitch only up to the point where you have just one more step to do to complete it. Grab the new yarn with your hook.

2 Pull the new yarn through both loops on your hook to complete the stitch. You've attached the new yarn.

3 Complete the row as usual, following the pattern directions.

Finishing School

When you've finished crocheting, there's only a little bit more to do before you've completed your project. First, you want to make sure your stitches won't unravel. Then you have to hide the yarn ends left over at the beginning and end of your work, and in the middle where you attached the new yarn.

FASTENING OFF

When you have finished crocheting, you'll need to secure the yarn end. This is called **fastening off.** To do this, first cut the yarn, leaving a 6-inch tail.

1 Remove your hook from the final stitch, pulling up the loop a little so it doesn't unravel. Pull the yarn tail through the loop.

2 Tug the yarn tail to tighten the knot.

WEAVING IN YARN ENDS

When a crochet project is done, you'll have "tails" of yarn hanging off the project where you finished one ball of yarn and began another one. Use a yarn needle to weave the yarn tails into your piece, hiding them inside the loops of the stitches. This is called **weaving in ends.**

Use a yarn needle to weave one yarn tail at a time into the crochet stitches on the side of your work that won't show (that's called the **wrong side**). It's a good idea to change direction frequently, in a zigzag or wavy pattern, so the tails will stay put.

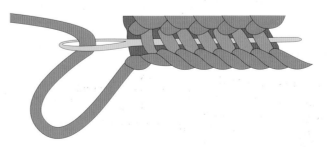

Gauge Is the Rage

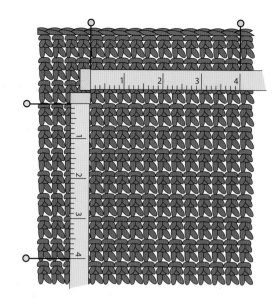

What is this "gauge" that is mentioned so often? **Gauge** is the number of stitches and rows that fit in a given area of crocheted fabric. You use this information to make sure your project will come out the right size. If the gauge you get as you crochet is different from the gauge called for in the pattern, your finished project will not be the same size the pattern specifies. For example, say a pattern specifies a gauge of 8 single crochets in 4 inches. If your own crochet fabric has 10 single crochet stitches in 4 inches, your finished piece will be narrower than the pattern requires; if your fabric has 6 stitches in 4 inches, your finished piece will be wider. The same goes for rows, which make up the length of the fabric.

Since gauge is so important, you should always make a **gauge swatch** before you begin a project. A swatch is a sample of what you'll be crocheting for the project. Use the same yarn, the same size crochet hook, and the same stitches specified in the pattern to make a 6-inch square. Fasten off. If your pattern calls for the finished piece to be blocked, block your swatch (see page 63).

Now measure your work. Lay a ruler or tape measure horizontally across a row. Count how many stitches fit in 4 inches in the middle of the swatch (not at the edges). Next, lay the ruler across the center of the swatch vertically and count how many rows fit in 4 inches. If your gauge matches the one specified in your pattern, you're good to go! If it doesn't, don't fret. If you have *too many* stitches or rows, make a new swatch with a *larger* hook. If you have *too few* stitches or rows, make a new swatch with a *smaller* hook. Then count again to see if it's right. If not, keep adjusting your hook size until you have the gauge called for in the pattern directions.

Oops, I Did It Again

"What if I make a mistake?!" you say. Here's what I say: embrace mistakes. All crocheters mess up, whether they're a newbie or an expert.

The most common problem is too many or too few stitches in a row—you accidentally increased or decreased somewhere. Before you pull out your stitches, take a good look at your work to see where the mistake occurred.

How does your fabric look? If you can barely see the mistake, you can simply increase or decrease in your current row to compensate. If, however, your fabric looks a little off or if you're just not happy with it, you can rip back to the row containing the error and rework it correctly. To rip back, just remove your hook from the current stitch and gently tug on the yarn to unravel the stitches. When you've ripped out the mistake, insert your hook into the active stitch and begin crocheting again from that point.

Autumn Striped Scarf

Pattern by Kim Werker

You've got new skills! Put them to work to make this super-simple scarf. When you're finished, you'll be a pro at making rows of half double crochet, changing colors (adding new skeins of yarn), and weaving in ends.

MATERIALS

* Lion Brand Wool-Ease Chunky yarn (80% acrylic, 20% wool; 153 yds/140m per 5 oz/140g): 1 skein each in Grass [Color A], Fisherman [Color B], and Pumpkin [Color C]
* Substitution: Approximately 100 yds/92m in Color A, 80 yds/73m in Color B, and 60 yds/55m in Color C of chunky weight yarn
* 8mm (size L) hook
* Yarn needle

FINISHED MEASUREMENTS

4½ inches wide x 68 inches long

GAUGE

6 half double crochets/ 8 rows = 4 inches

(Note: Gauge is not important for this scarf.)

68"

4½"

PATTERN

* With Color A, chain 138.
* Row 1: Half double crochet into the third chain from your hook, half double crochet into each chain across. Chain 2, turn your work so the turning chain you just made is now on the right if you're right-handed, or on the left if you're left-handed. The turning chain does not count as a stitch in this pattern, so don't skip the first stitch, and make sure to count your stitches at the end of the row. You should have 136 stitches in every row—136 stitches total.
* Row 2: Half double crochet into each stitch across the row until you have just 1 more stitch to make. Yarn over, insert your hook into the last stitch and draw up a loop. There are now 3 loops on your hook, and your stitch is one step away from being completed. Leaving a 6-inch tail, cut the Color A yarn. Drop Color A and pick up Color B. Leave a 6-inch yarn tail and complete the final stitch with Color B (see page 31 for more on how to attach new yarn). Chain 2, turn.
* Row 3: Half double crochet into each stitch across the row, changing to Color C in the final stitch. Chain 2, turn.
* Row 4: Half double crochet into each stitch across the row. Chain 2, turn.
* Row 5: Half double crochet into each stitch across the row, changing to Color B in the final stitch. Chain 2, turn.
* Row 6: Half double crochet into each stitch across the row, changing to Color A in the final stitch. Chain 2, turn.
* Row 7: Half double crochet into each stitch across the row. Chain 2, turn.
* Row 8: Half double crochet into each stitch across the row.
* Fasten off and weave in the yarn ends.

Tip

If you want to make a longer scarf, begin with more than 138 chains. If you want a shorter scarf, make fewer chains. Then just follow the instructions as they're written!

Moving in Circles

Who said crochet can only be done in squares and rectangles? One of the greatest things about crochet is that you can do it in a circle. All you need to know is how to add stitches to your work.

On the Increase

Making two or more stitches into the same place increases the total number of stitches in your work. By increasing, you can shape your crocheted fabric in lots of cool ways. Here's how to increase by one stitch (this works with any crochet stitch!).

1 Insert your hook in the same stitch you just worked into.

2 Complete the stitch as usual. You've now made two stitches in the same stitch.

Take a close look at the row you've just completed and you can see where you worked two stitches in the same place.

Getting in Shape

So, what kinds of shapes can you make with increasing? By placing an increase in the first and last stitches of a row, you can make a triangle or a trapezoid. By placing increases at regular intervals when you crochet in the round (see page 38), you'll make a circle that lays flat. If you increase repeatedly into every stitch of your work, you'll end up with a funky ruffle.

Many of the projects in this book use increases to shape things such as the sole of a slipper (see **Ruby Slippers** on page 82), the armholes of a vest (see **Honor Roll Vest** on page 90), or the top of a hat (see **Chunky Hat** on page 40).

Merry Go Round

Crocheting **in the round** is just what it sounds like. Instead of making rows, you crochet around and around in a circle or an oval. You usually don't turn your work after each round like you do with rows—you just keep going in the same direction, making your next round on top of the one you just finished. Increasing is an important part of crocheting in the round. It makes your circle grow bigger with every round so it lays nice and flat—at least until you don't want it to be flat anymore!

1 To work in the round, start out with a chain—the number of chain stitches you make will be specified in the pattern you're following. In this example, it's a chain of six.

2 To join the chain, make a slip stitch in the very first chain to form a ring.

3 To make your first round, insert your hook into the center of the ring—not into an individual chain stitch. You are going to work each of the next stitches around the ring itself.

4 When you have gone all the way around, join the last stitch to the first with a slip stitch. You have now completed one round.

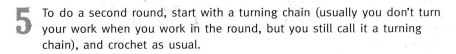

5 To do a second round, start with a turning chain (usually you don't turn your work when you work in the round, but you still call it a turning chain), and crochet as usual.

Edgy Behavior

As you've probably already discovered, you can stick your crochet hook pretty much anywhere. This includes the sides of rows, not just the tops of stitches. See where I'm going here? You can work really awesome borders and edges around all the sides of your work!

BASIC EDGING

The simplest edging you can do is to work a row (or more) of slip stitch or single crochet around your piece. You can do this whether your piece is round or rectangular.

ON A ROUND Join the new yarn where you fastened off the last round. Chain 1, then work a single crochet in the same stitch you joined the yarn to.

* Edging round: Work 1 single crochet in each stitch around, making the same number of increases (working 2 single crochets in the same stitch) as you did in the last round of the piece. For example, if you wanted to add an edging to the Chunky Hat on page 40, you would make 8 increases in the edging round, just like you made 8 increases in each round of the hat.

* Slip stitch in the first edge stitch to join the round. You can fasten off, or chain 1 and continue to work a second round of single crochet for a wider edging.

AROUND A RECTANGLE Starting in the top right corner, (if you're a rightie, or in the top left if you're a leftie) join the new yarn. Chain 1, then work 1 single crochet in the same stitch you joined the yarn to.

* Edging row: Work 1 single crochet in each stitch across the top of the piece until only 1 stitch remains to be worked. Work 3 single crochets into the final stitch for the corner (this turns your work around the corner).

* Don't flip your work around as you would if you were going to work a new row, but rotate it 90 degrees so you can keep crocheting along the next side. Work 1 single crochet into each space between the rows. Work 3 stitches into the final space for the corner. Continue working around the shape until you get back to the beginning of the border.

* Slip stitch in the first edge stitch to join the border. You can fasten off, or chain 1 and continue to work a second round of single crochet for a wider border.

PICOT EDGING

Picots are easy to make. You just make a short chain and slip stitch into the bottom of it to make a little ball of yarn. You need an odd number of stitches to work a symmetrical picot edging. Join the new yarn and make a single crochet in the first stitch.

* Picot row: *Chain 3, and make a slip stitch in the first chain (the one farthest from your hook). Skip 1 stitch, and make a single crochet in the next stitch*. Repeat from * to *, working all around the item. Fasten off.

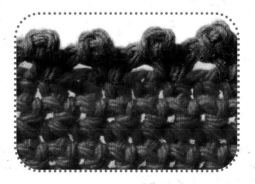

Chunky Hat

Pattern by Kim Werker

SKILLS Chain, slip stitch, single crochet, double crochet, increasing, working in the round, joining new yarn, weaving in ends

This is the simplest hat around, and it's SO cute to boot! It's made in the round in double crochet stitches, with a simple single crochet edging around the brim. You start out making a flat circle, then you work even rounds without increasing to make the circle turn into the shape of a hat. Once you get the hang of it, you'll be able to whip one up super fast for each of your friends—in different colors, of course!

MATERIALS

* Lion Brand Wool-Ease Chunky yarn (80% acrylic, 20% wool; 153 yds/140m per 5 oz/140g): 1 skein each in Fisherman [Color A] and Pumpkin [Color B]
* Substitution: Approximately 110 yds/100m in Color A and 30 yds/27m in Color B of chunky weight yarn
* 8mm (size L) hook, or size needed to obtain gauge
* Yarn needle

FINISHED MEASUREMENTS

18 inches around (unstretched); 7½ inches from brim to top

GAUGE

7 double crochets/5½ rows = 4 inches

PATTERN

* This hat is made of double crochet stitches worked in the round. You make only two turning chains (instead of the three usually made for double crochet), and the turning chain does not count as a stitch. This helps to hide the join in each round and makes a prettier circle.

* With Color A, chain 4. Slip stitch in the first chain to form a ring.

* Round 1: Chain 2. Work 8 double crochets into the center of the ring. (It may seem a little crowded but just push the stitches over to make room for more.) Slip stitch in the first double crochet to join the round—8 double crochets total.

* Round 2: Chain 2. Double crochet in the same stitch you just slip stitched into, double crochet in the next stitch, work 2 double crochets into each remaining stitch in the round. Slip stitch in the first double crochet to join—16 double crochets total.

* Round 3: Chain 2. Double crochet in the same stitch you just slip stitched into, double crochet in the next stitch, *double crochet in the next stitch, work 2 double crochets in the next stitch*. Repeat from * to * around. Slip stitch in the first double crochet to join—24 double crochets total.

* Round 4: Chain 2. Double crochet in the same stitch you just slip stitched into, double crochet in the next stitch, work 2 double crochets in the next stitch, *double crochet in each of the next 2 stitches, work 2 double crochets in the next stitch*. Repeat from * to * around. Slip stitch in the first double crochet to join—32 double crochets total.

* Rounds 5–8: Chain 2. Double crochet in the same stitch you just slip stitched into, double crochet in each stitch around. Slip stitch in the first double crochet to join.

* Round 9: Chain 2. Double crochet in the same stitch you just slip stitched into, double crochet in each stitch around. Changing to Color B, slip stitch in the first double crochet to join.

* Rounds 10–11: Chain 1. Single crochet in the same stitch you just slip stitched into, single crochet in each stitch around. Slip stitch in the first single crochet to join.

* Fasten off and weave in the yarn ends.

Tip

When a pattern says to "work even" it simply means to continue crocheting in the established stitch pattern without making any increases or decreases.

Boil It Down

No doubt you figured decreasing would come after increasing, right? You got it! It's useful to be able to subtract stitches from a row or round, and you can practice by making a super-practical case for your sunglasses.

Less Is More

Just as you shaped your crocheted fabric by increasing, or adding stitches, you can also shape by decreasing, or subtracting stitches. Here are two ways to subtract stitches from your work.

WORKING STITCHES TOGETHER

The most common way to decrease is to do what we call working two stitches together, and it produces a gradual, slanting decrease. Essentially, you make one stitch where there were two in the previous row or round. Here's how to decrease by one stitch (this can be adapted to any crochet stitch).

1 Work the next stitch only up to the point where you have two loops remaining on your hook (in other words, work the stitch until you only have to do one more step to complete it).

2 Insert your hook in the next stitch, and again work the stitch only up to the point at which you have to do one more step to complete it. Because you already had two loops on your hook, you now have three loops.

3 Yarn over and pull the yarn through all three loops. You have just worked two stitches together. Look closely, and you will see that there is only one V at the top of the two stitches you worked together.

LEAVING STITCHES UNWORKED

There's also a more dramatic way to decrease the number of stitches in your work—it's by simply leaving them unworked.

AT THE BEGINNING OF A ROW At the beginning of a row, work a slip stitch into each stitch you want to "skip." The slip stitch is so short, the stitches will appear to be unworked. After slip stitching in the stitches, make a chain to create the height you need to start making the next stitches (see page 30) and continue across the row as instructed by your pattern.

AT THE END OF A ROW
At the end of a row, simply stop crocheting and make a turning chain, leaving the rest of the row's stitches unworked. Turn your work as you normally would, and continue with the next row as instructed by your pattern.

Seams So Easy

Not all crochet projects are made in one piece—and some that are made in one piece still need to be folded and sewn up. Most of the time you hold the two crocheted pieces with their right sides together, so the seams you sew will be hidden on the inside of the project when you turn it right side out. Sometimes, though, a seam can be used for decoration. In that case you place the wrong sides together to keep the seam on the outside of the finished item.

In either case, if you want the seam to be subtle or even entirely hidden, use the same yarn you used to crochet the project. If you want to add some flair, especially if you're working the seam on the outside of the project, use yarn in a complementary color.

WHIP STITCH SEAM

Whip stitching is an easy way to sew two pieces together. It's such a pretty stitch, though, you may just want to make it on the outside of your work!

Insert the needle from front to back through the first stitch of both pieces and draw the yarn through, leaving a 6-inch tail. Bring the needle back around to the front, and insert it from front to back through the next stitch of both pieces. Pull the yarn through. Repeat.

SLIP STITCH SEAM

You can also crochet your pieces together. Crocheted seams are very strong, but they can also be a bit bulky. If you used a chunky yarn to crochet with, you may want to use a matching thinner yarn to make your seam.

Attach your seaming yarn to the hook with a slip knot. Holding the pieces with the right sides together, insert your hook in the first stitch of both pieces, and make a slip stitch. Continue along the edge, making slip stitches through both pieces.

SINGLE CROCHET SEAM

The single crochet seam is bulky and is often left on the outside of a finished piece because it adds a raised, decorative detail.

Attach the seaming yarn to the hook with a slip knot. Holding the pieces with the wrong sides together (so the seam will show on the outside), insert your hook in the first stitch of both pieces, and make a single crochet stitch. Continue along the edge, making single crochet stitches through both pieces.

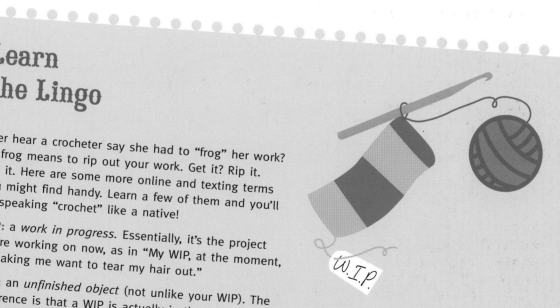

Learn the Lingo

Ever hear a crocheter say she had to "frog" her work? To frog means to rip out your work. Get it? Rip it. Rip it. Here are some more online and texting terms you might find handy. Learn a few of them and you'll be speaking "crochet" like a native!

WIP: a *work in progress*. Essentially, it's the project you're working on now, as in "My WIP, at the moment, is making me want to tear my hair out."

UFO: an *unfinished object* (not unlike your WIP). The difference is that a WIP is actually in the works and a UFO might be a project that's been languishing under your bed for a few months. Don't be embarrassed! Most crocheters have a few UFOs hanging around.

FO: a—drum roll, please!—*finished object*. You know, from the last time your mom made you clean under your bed and you discovered that long-lost scarf you finally decided to finish!

Shelter-Your-Shades Case

Pattern by Kim Werker

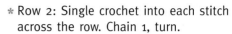
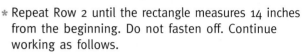

SKILLS Chain, slip stitch, single crochet, decreasing, weaving in ends

Nobody likes wearing scratched-up sunglasses. Use this super-soft case to keep yours safe when they're not on your face! The whole case is crocheted in one piece, then folded up and seamed on the outside for decoration.

MATERIALS

* Lion Brand Microspun yarn (100% micro-fiber acrylic; 168 yds/154m per 2.50 oz/70g): 1 skein in Mango [Color A] and leftover scrap amount in Turquoise [Color B]
* Substitution: Approximately 100 yds/90m of worsted weight yarn
* 5mm (size H) hook, or size needed to obtain gauge
* Yarn needle
* Straight pin
* 1 button
* Sewing needle and thread to match yarn

FINISHED MEASUREMENTS

3½ inches wide x 6½ inches tall

GAUGE

5 single crochets/ 5 rows = 1 inch

PATTERN

* With Color A, chain 16.
* Row 1: Single crochet into the second chain from your hook, single

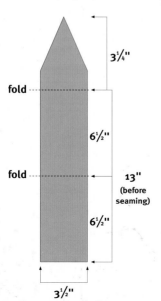

crochet into each chain across. Chain 1, turn—15 single crochets total.

* Row 2: Single crochet into each stitch across the row. Chain 1, turn.
* Repeat Row 2 until the rectangle measures 14 inches from the beginning. Do not fasten off. Continue working as follows.

Make the flap

* Row 1 (decrease row): Work 2 single crochets together over the first 2 stitches (1 decrease made), single crochet across the row until only 2 stitches remain, work 2 single crochets together over the last 2 stitches (second decrease made). Chain 1, turn.
* Row 2: Single crochet in each stitch across the row. Chain 1, turn.
* Repeat Flap Rows 1 and 2 six times, until only 3 stitches remain. Chain 1, turn. Work the last 3 stitches together in the same way you work 2 stitches together: Insert your hook into the first stitch and draw up a loop, insert your hook into the second stitch and draw up a loop, insert your hook into the third stitch and draw up a loop. Now there are 4 loops on your hook. Yarn over and draw the yarn through all 4 loops. Now there's only 1 stitch left.

Make the button loop

* Chain 7, slip stitch in the first single crochet. Fasten off and weave in the yarn ends.

FINISHING

1. Fold the case so the beginning end (the one with the foundation chain) lines up with the top just below the flap. Using Color B and a yarn needle, whip stitch each of the long sides together.

2. Weave in the yarn ends.

3. Close the flap and use a straight pin to mark the place opposite the button loop where the button will go. Using a sewing needle and thread, sew on the button.

fold

The Patterns!

You've made it this far—you must be itching to dive in! This chapter includes twelve way fun patterns to keep you busy for weeks on end!

Lacy Choker

Pattern by Dora Ohrenstein

SKILLS Chain, slip stitch, single crochet, double crochet, working in the back loop only, weaving in ends

Need an eye-catching accessory for the weekend? This little neck-hugger will work up in an hour or less. No special gizmos needed to close it; simply tie the ends in the back. You can try this design in any DK weight yarn.

MATERIALS

* Black choker: 1 skein Berroco Metallic FX yarn (85% rayon, 15% metallic; 85 yds/78m per 7/8 oz/25g) in Silver Black #1004
* White choker: 1 ball Berroco Zodiac yarn (53% cotton, 47% nylon; 97 yds/90m per 1.75 oz/50g) in Luna #9607
* Substitution: Approximately 20 yds/18m of DK weight yarn
* 2.75 mm (size C) hook, or size needed to obtain gauge
* Stitch marker
* Yarn needle

FINISHED MEASUREMENTS

Black choker: 26½ inches long x 1⅛ inches wide, including ties

White choker: 28½ inches long x 1⅛ inches wide, including ties

GAUGE

Black choker: 4 pattern repeats = 4¾ inches

White choker: 4 pattern repeats = 5 inches

PATTERN

* Chain 5, slip stitch in the first chain (end loop made), chain 40 (one tie chain made), mark the last chain with a stitch marker, then make 68 additional chains. Turn.

* Row 1: Single crochet in the *back loop only* (see page 29) of the second chain and in the *back loop only* of each chain across the row up to the marked chain—67 single crochets. Turn.

* Row 2: Chain 1. Single crochet in the first single crochet, *chain 3, skip 2 single crochets, double crochet in the next single crochet, chain 3, skip 2 single crochets, single crochet in the next single crochet*. You have completed 1 pattern repeat. Repeat from * to * across until you have a total of 11 pattern repeats. Turn.

* Row 3: Chain 5 (counts as double crochet plus chain-2), *picot in next double crochet (see box), chain 2, double crochet in the next single crochet*. Repeat from * to * across the row. Fasten off.

FINISHING

To make the tie chain on the opposite end, attach the yarn in top of the last single crochet of Row 1. Chain 45, slip stitch in the fifth chain from your hook. Fasten off. Weave in all yarn ends. For best results, weave the yarn ends of the tie chains into the bumps on the underside of the chains.

MAKING VARIATIONS

The choker requires 20 yards of yarn, so it's the perfect project for thinner leftover yarns. If you want to try a thicker yarn, make a test sample first with 3 or 4 pattern repeats (the part between *s in Rows 2 and 3) to see what your new gauge is. Then measure around your neck to decide how long you want the necklace to be and make the appropriate number of chains.

For each pattern repeat, you will need 6 chains in Row 1, plus 2 chains at the end. So, to figure out how many chains you should start with, just multiply the number of patterns by 6, then add 2. For example, if your new version requires only 10 repeats, then 10 x 6 = 60 chains. Add the 2 at the end = 62. So you should begin with 62 chains (not counting the tie chains).

A Picot

To make a picot, work [single crochet, chain 3, single crochet] in the designated stitch.

Hook Roll

Pattern by Lauren Irving

SKILLS Chain, slip stitch, single crochet, double crochet, working in the round, weaving in ends, seaming

Stop wasting time digging around the bottom of your bag for another missing crochet hook. Whip up this quick and easy hook roll to keep all of your hooks, yarn needles—even scissors and stitch markers—together and organized.

MATERIALS

* Elmore-Pisgah Peaches & Crème yarn (100% cotton; 122 yds/111.6m per 2.5 oz/71g): 1 ball each in Sunburst #11 [Color A], Shocking Pink #131 [Color B], and Yellow #10 [Color C]
* Substitution: Approximately 112 yds/103m in Color A and 2 yds/2m in Colors B and C of worsted weight cotton
* 5 mm (size H) hook, or size needed to obtain gauge
* Tape measure or ruler
* Yarn needle
* ½ yard of ¼-inch-wide polyester ribbon
* Embroidery needle
* Sewing thread to match Color B
* ⅜-inch or ½-inch buttons for decoration (optional)

FINISHED MEASUREMENTS

9 inches long x 8 inches wide when opened

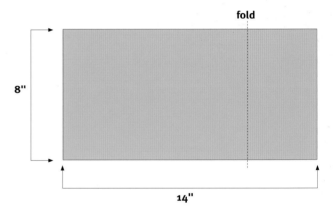

GAUGE

14 single crochets/18 rows = 4 inches

PATTERN

* With Color A, chain 29.
* Row 1: Single crochet in the second chain from your hook and in each chain across—28 single crochets total. Turn.
* Row 2: Chain 1. Single crochet in each stitch across the row. Turn.
* Repeat Row 2 for 14 inches. Fasten off and weave in the yarn ends.

more ↵

Make the flowers (Make 2 in Color B and 2 in Color C)

* With Color B or Color C, chain 4. Slip stitch into the fourth chain from the hook to form a ring.

* Round 1: *Chain 2, work 2 double crochets into the center of the ring, chain 2*. Slip stitch into the ring (one petal made). Repeat from * to * three more times—4 petals total.

* Fasten off, leaving an 8-inch tail to sew the flower to the hook roll.

FINISHING

Make the pockets

1. Place the crocheted rectangle in front of you with one short side at the bottom. Using a tape measure or ruler as a guide, fold the bottom edge up onto the rectangle, creating a 5-inch-deep pocket. Using the yarn needle and Color A, whip stitch (see page 44) both side edges of the pocket together.

2. Make five ¾-inch hook pockets and two 1½-inch hook pockets as follows: To create the first pocket, thread the yarn needle with Color A again and starting at the bottom right corner, bring the yarn through the top layer of the first 3 stitches along the bottom edge. Then, using a running stitch, sew a seam going straight up to the top of the pocket, working through both layers of crochet. You have made one pocket.

3. For the next pocket, bring the yarn through the top layer of the next 3 stitches to the left—make sure you do not sew the hook pockets closed at the top! Using a running stitch, sew a seam, going back down to the bottom, working through both layers of crochet. Make three more pockets the same way.

4. For the next pocket, bring the yarn through the top layer of 6 stitches, then use a running stitch to sew a seam, going back down to the bottom, working through both layers of crochet. Make another pocket that is 6 stitches wide. Fasten off and weave in the yarn ends.

Gotta Run? Make a running stitch by weaving the yarn needle in and out of both layers of fabric at equal intervals.

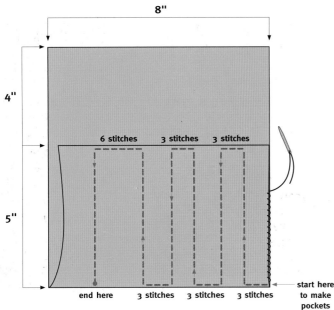

8"

4"

5"

6 stitches 3 stitches 3 stitches

end here 3 stitches 3 stitches 3 stitches → start here to make pockets

Add the ribbon closure

1. Fold the top flap down to the top of the pockets, and then fold the hook roll in half.

2. Fold the ribbon in half. Line up the center of the ribbon with the center back of the hook roll, and sew the ribbon in place using an embroidery needle threaded with two strands of sewing thread and making sure you do not sew the hook pockets closed.

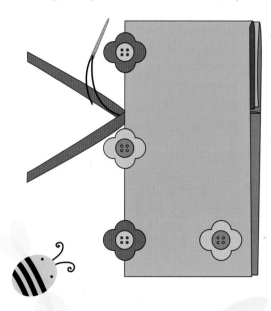

Sew on the flowers

1. Fold the hook roll into thirds.

2. With embroidery needle threaded with two strands of sewing thread, sew three flowers to the back of the roll where you attached the ribbon closure, making sure you do not sew the hook pockets closed. Sew buttons to the center of the flowers if you like.

3. Sew one flower to the front of the roll where you tie the ribbon closed.

Store It All

The hook roll can hold many of your hooks and supplies. Each 3-stitch pocket can hold one large hook or two or three smaller hooks. Each 6-stitch pocket can hold a flexible tape measure, small scissors, or a couple of extra-large hooks. The fronts of the pockets can hold your yarn needles if you weave the needles into the crochet stitches. Attach your stitch markers by clipping them to the stitches. The flap folds down over the tops of the hooks to prevent them from falling out when the case is closed.

Crochet-Anywhere Tote

Pattern by Lauren Irving

SKILLS Chain, single crochet, joining new yarn, weaving in ends, seaming

Now there's no excuse not to have your crochet with you all the time! Make this cute bag to show off your new skills and keep your projects in one place. It's large enough for a few skeins of yarn, pattern books, hooks, and the matching hook roll. Toss your cell phone and lip gloss into the side pockets and you're good to go.

MATERIALS

* Elmore-Pisgah Peaches & Crème yarn (100% cotton; 122 yds/111.6m per 2.5 oz/71g): 4 balls in Shocking Pink #131 [Color A]; 1 ball each in Yellow #10 [Color B] and Sunburst #11 [Color C]
* Substitution: Approximately 440 yds/402m in Color A, 175 yds/160m in Color B, and 50 yds/46m in Color C of worsted weight cotton
* 5mm (size H) hook, or size needed to obtain gauge
* 2 stitch markers
* Pins
* Yarn needle
* One ½-inch-diameter x 36-inch-long wooden dowel, cut in half (by the hardware or home improvement store where you buy it)
* 220-grit sandpaper
* 12-inch x 18-inch sheet of Darice plastic canvas Clear Ultra Stiff (available in crafts stores) or foam core board or heavy-duty cardboard

FINISHED MEASUREMENTS

15½ inches wide x 10 inches high x 4½ inches deep

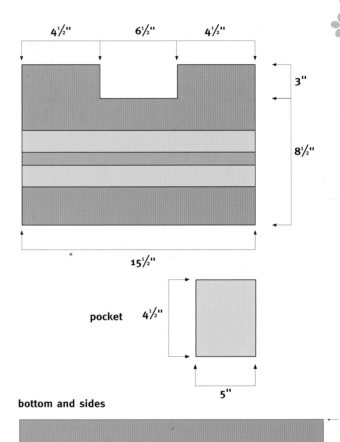

pocket

bottom and sides

GAUGE

14 single crochets/18 rows = 4 inches

more

PATTERN

The body (Make 2)

* With Color A, chain 57.

* Row 1: Single crochet in the second chain from your hook and in each chain across—56 stitches total. Turn.

* Row 2: Chain 1. Single crochet in each stitch across the row. Turn.

* Rows 3–15: Repeat Row 2, changing to Color B in the last stitch of Row 15. Turn.

* Rows 16–21: Repeat Row 2, changing to Color C in the last stitch of Row 21. Turn.

* Rows 22–25: Repeat Row 2, changing to Color B in the last stitch of Row 25. Turn.

* Row 26–31: Repeat Row 2, changing to Color A in the last stitch of Row 31. Turn.

* Row 32–40: Repeat Row 2. Place a stitch marker at each end of the last row. Turn.

Make the first handle cover

* Row 1: Chain 1. Single crochet in each of the next 18 stitches—18 stitches total. Turn.

* Row 2: Chain 1. Single crochet in each stitch across the row. Turn.

* Rows 3–12: Repeat Row 2.

* Fasten off, leaving a 12-inch yarn tail to sew the handle cover to the body of the bag later.

Make the second handle cover

* Row 1: Place the body of the bag so the handle cover you just worked is on your right. Count 18 stitches from the left edge of the bag. Join Color A in the 18th stitch. Chain 1, and single crochet in the same stitch. (Flip the sides if you're a leftie.)

* Single crochet in each of the last 17 stitches—18 stitches total. Turn.

* Row 2: Chain 1. Single crochet in each stitch across the row. Turn.

* Rows 3–12: Repeat Row 2.

* Fasten off, leaving a 12-inch yarn tail to sew the handle cover to the body of the bag later.

Sides and bottom (Make 1)

* With Color A, chain 18.

* Row 1: Single crochet in the second chain from your hook and in each chain across— 17 stitches total. Turn.

* Row 2: Chain 1. Single crochet in each stitch across the row. Turn.

* Repeat Row 2 for 34 inches. Fasten off and weave in the yarn ends.

Side pockets (Make 2)

* With Color B, chain 16.

* Row 1: Single crochet in the second chain from your hook and in each chain across—15 stitches total. Turn.

* Row 2: Chain 1. Single crochet in each stitch across the row. Turn.

* Repeat Row 2 for 4½ inches. Fasten off, leaving a 15-inch yarn tail to sew the pockets to the body of the bag later.

FINISHING

Sew the bag together

1. Pin the side-and-bottom panel to one body panel, lining up each short end of the side with the marked row on the body. Check to make sure the side panel fits all the way around the body before sewing; if it doesn't fit, add or pull out rows of the side panel as needed.

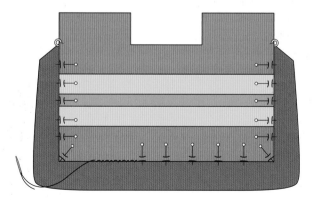

2. Thread a yarn needle with Color A. Whip stitch (see page 44) one piece of the body and one edge of the side/bottom panel together, easing the edge of the side panel around the corners as needed.

3. Whip stitch the second piece of the body to the opposite edge of the side/bottom panel in the same manner.

Attach the handles

1. Thread the yarn needle with the yarn tail end from a handle cover. Fold the handle cover in half, and whip stitch the free end to the inside of the bag. Repeat for the other three handle cover ends. Turn the bag right side out.

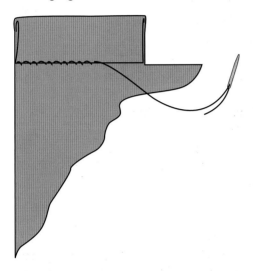

2. Slip the dowels through the handle covers you just made.

Attach the side pockets

1. Thread the yarn needle with the yarn tail from one side pocket. With the yarn tail at the top, pin one pocket piece to the side of the bag, lining up the bottom of the pocket with the bottom edge of the bag.

2. Whip stitch around three sides of the pocket, leaving the top edge open. Sew the second pocket to the opposite side of the bag.

Insert the base support

1. Cut the plastic canvas into two 15½-inch x 4½-inch pieces. Cut carefully so you have clean edges.

2. Place one piece of plastic canvas on top of the other and whip stitch around all four edges with Color A to bind them together. (If you're using foam core or cardboard, use a heavy tape, such as duct tape, to bind the pieces.)

3. Place the plastic canvas in the bottom of the bag. Sew several rows of a long running stitch to secure the plastic canvas to the bottom of the bag (or place the foam core board or cardboard in the bottom; there is no need to stitch it in place).

Gidget Bucket Hat

Pattern by Chloe Nightingale

SKILLS Chain, slip stitch, single crochet, double crochet, treble crochet, increasing, working in the round, weaving in ends

They call it a bucket hat—we call it cool. Cotton yarn makes this hat ideal for spring and summer. It's the perfect warm-weather accessory, or a great cover-up for those disastrous, humid hair days.

MATERIALS

* Elmore-Pisgah Peaches & Créme 4-ply cotton yarn (100% cotton; 120 yds/110m per 2.5 oz/71g): 2 balls in Apple Green #51 [Color A]; and 1 ball each in Baby Pink #47 [Color B], Sunburst #11 [Color C], and Peacock #19 [Color D]
* Substitution: Approximately 240 yds/220m in Color A, 25 yds/23m in Color B, 5 yds/4.5m in Color C, and 10 yds/9m in Color D
* 3.75mm (size F) hook, or size needed to obtain gauge
* Stitch marker
* Yarn needle

FINISHED MEASUREMENTS

8 inches from the top to the bottom of the brim

20 inches in circumference at the band; 29 inches in circumference at the bottom of the brim

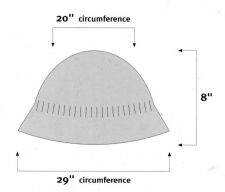

20" circumference

8"

29" circumference

GAUGE

18 single crochets/17 rows = 4 inches

(Note: The hat may crochet up tightly at this gauge, but it will stretch to fit most heads.)

PATTERN

(Note: Do not join the rounds; you will work in a spiral. Place a stitch marker in the first stitch to mark the start of the round. When you reach the stitch marker again, remove it and work the stitch as directed, then immediately place the marker into the stitch you just made to mark the start of the next round.)

* With Color A, chain 3. Slip stitch in the first chain to form a ring.
* Round 1: Work 8 single crochets into the ring—8 stitches total.
* Round 2: Work 2 single crochets in each stitch around—16 stitches total.
* Round 3: Work 2 single crochets in each stitch around—32 stitches total.
* Rounds 4–6: Single crochet in each stitch around.
* Round 7: Work 2 single crochets in each stitch around—64 stitches total.
* Rounds 8–13: Single crochet in each stitch around.
* Round 14: Single crochet in each of the next 2 stitches, *single crochet in each of the next 2 stitches, work 2 single crochets in the next stitch*. Repeat from * to * around, ending with a single crochet in each of the last 2 stitches—84 stitches total.
* Rounds 15–24: Single crochet in each stitch around.
* Round 25: Chain 3, (counts as a double crochet), treble crochet in each stitch around, ending with a double crochet in the last stitch.
* Round 26: Single crochet in the top chain of the chain-3 from the previous round, single crochet in each stitch around.

more

- Round 27: *Single crochet in the next stitch, work 2 single crochets in the next stitch*. Repeat from * to * around—126 stitches total.
- Rounds 28–32: Single crochet in each stitch around, ending with a slip stitch in the last stitch.
- Fasten off and weave in the yarn ends.

Choose your band

Here are three different types of hatbands to choose from. Make up several in your favorite colors and then change the band to match your outfit or your mood!

Left to right: Flower hatband, simple hatband, ribbon hatband.

Simple hatband (shown in orange and on model)

- With Color C, chain 150.
- Fasten off. Weave the band through the treble crochet stitches of the hat and tie into a bow.

Ribbon hatband (shown in pink)

- With Color B, chain 201.
- Row 1: Single crochet in the second stitch from your hook and in each chain across—200 stitches total. Turn.
- Row 2: Chain 1. Single crochet in each stitch across.

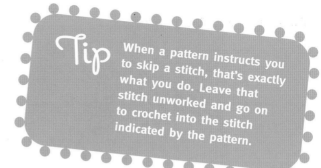

Tip When a pattern instructs you to skip a stitch, that's exactly what you do. Leave that stitch unworked and go on to crochet into the stitch indicated by the pattern.

- Fasten off and weave in the yarn ends. Weave the band through the treble crochet stitches of the hat and tie into a bow.

Flower hatband (shown in blue)

- Start making the flower:
- With Color D, chain 6. Slip stitch in the first chain to form a ring.
- Round 1: Work 12 single crochets into the ring. Do not join the round—12 stitches total.
- Round 2: Chain 6, skip the first stitch, single crochet in the next stitch, *chain 6, skip the next stitch, single crochet in the next stitch*. Repeat from * to * around, to form 6 petals total. (The flower isn't finished just yet—you'll add another round to it after you crochet the stem, which is the band that is wrapped around your hat. The stem is connected to the flower, so do not fasten off.)
- Make the stem: Starting right where you left off, chain 100.
- Row 1: Single crochet in the 11th chain from your hook and in each chain across until you reach the flower. This creates a stem with a chain-loop on the end opposite the flower. This completes the stem.

* Finish the flower: Round 3: Work 6 single crochets into each chain-6 space of the flower. Slip stitch in the first stitch of the stem.

* Fasten off and weave in the yarn ends.

* Weave the stem through the treble crochet stitches of the hat, and fasten it in place by pulling the flower through the chain-loop on the other end of the stem.

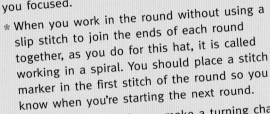

Round 'n' Round

Is your head spinning? Here are some tips for working in the round that will help keep you focused.

* When you work in the round without using a slip stitch to join the ends of each round together, as you do for this hat, it is called working in a spiral. You should place a stitch marker in the first stitch of the round so you know when you're starting the next round.

* For projects in which you make a turning chain at the beginning of each round, it's easy to see when you get to the end of the round because the turning chain is higher than the stitches from the previous round, so you might not need a marker.

* And now you might ask, If you don't turn your work when you crochet in the round, why do you make a turning chain? Good question. In this case, "turning chain" is a total misnomer. Even though you don't flip your work around to go back in the other direction, you still need to make up for the height of the stitches in the round you're about to crochet, so you make chains to accomplish this. We call them turning chains even though there's no turning involved.

Be a Blockhead

When you crochet with natural fiber yarns, you can have quite a lot of control over how the fabric is shaped and how it drapes when you're done crocheting. You exercise this control by **blocking** your project. In the case of lace, blocking can help to open up the stitches so the pattern looks crisp and lays beautifully. You can also block solid fabrics to make them lay flat if they curl up a little at the edges.

Lay your project out on a firm, flat, cushioned surface such as your bed, a clean carpet, or a few folded towels. Using rust-proof straight pins, pin the project into the shape you want and follow the schematic drawing and measurement of each piece given in your pattern to pin it to the proper size if the finished dimensions are important (such as for a sweater or a vest). For the lace scarf, you can stretch the scarf widthwise and lengthwise to make it look perfect. Lightly spray water on the project using a spray bottle. Allow the project to air-dry (overnight, if necessary). When you take out the pins, your project will retain the shape. It's like magic!

Workin'-for-You Scarf

Pattern by Kim Werker

SKILLS Chain, double crochet, weaving in ends

This scarf works for you in whatever yarn you like! This project shows what the very same pattern looks like when made with yarns of different colors and textures. And it introduces lace, one of crochet's best features. This super simple pattern is called chevron lace and was inspired by a stitch found in a stitch dictionary (see page 94).

MATERIALS

* Blue Version: 1 skein Brown Sheep Company Cotton Fleece yarn (80% cotton/20% merino wool; 215 yds/197m per 3.5 oz/100g) in My Blue Heaven #CW-560
* Substitution: Approximately 120 yds/110m of light worsted weight yarn (yarn weight 3)
* Orange Version: 1 ball Crystal Palace Yarns Merino Stripes yarn (90% merino wool/ 10% acrylic; 115 yds/106m per 50g) in #27
* Substitution: Approximately 115 yds/106m of worsted weight yarn with a similar texture (yarn weight 4)
* 6mm (size J) hook
* Yarn needle

FINISHED MEASUREMENTS

6 inches wide x 38 inches long (unblocked)

38"

6"

GAUGE

3 double crochets/1 row = 1 inch (unblocked)

SPECIAL NOTES

"Skip 2 stitches or chains" means to leave the next 2 stitches or chains unworked and to make your next stitch into the third stitch or chain from your hook.

In this pattern, the turning chain is worked at the beginning of a row instead of the end. That's because it counts as a double crochet stitch. When the pattern says to "work 2 double crochets into the top of the turning chain," you should make the stitches into the top chain of the 3 chains that make up the turning chain from the previous row.

PATTERN

* Chain 22.

* Row 1: Double crochet into the third chain from your hook, double crochet into each of the next 3 chains, skip 2 chains, double crochet into each of the next 4 chains, chain 2, double crochet into each of the next 4 chains, skip 2 chains, double crochet into each of the next 3 chains, work 2 double crochets into the last chain, turn.

* Row 2: Chain 3 (the turning chain counts as the first double crochet), double crochet into the first stitch, double crochet into each of the next 3 stitches, skip 2 stitches, double crochet into each of the next 3 stitches, [double crochet, chain 2, double crochet] into the space left by the chain-2 from the previous row, double crochet into each of the next 3 stitches, skip 2 stitches, double crochet into each of the next 3 stitches, work 2 double crochets into the top of the turning chain, turn.

* Repeat Row 2 until your scarf is the desired length or you run out of yarn.

* Fasten off and weave in the yarn ends. Block (see page 63).

Fingerless Street Mitts

Pattern by Amy Swenson

> **SKILLS** Chain, slip stitch, half double crochet, decreasing, working in the round, attaching new yarn, weaving in ends

Fingerless mitts provide a bit of warmth without sacrificing your cool. They keep your fingers free so you can keep on texting, dialing your cell, or turning up your iPod. Each mitten is worked from the fingers to the wrist, using a non-stretchy foundation round so the mitts won't flare out at the fingers.

MATERIALS

* Cascade 220 yarn (100% wool; 220 yds/201m per 3.5 oz/100g): 1 skein each in #8400 [Color A] and #2450 [Color B]
* Substitution: Approximately 50 yds/46m each of 2 colors of worsted weight yarn
* 4mm (size G) hook, or size needed to obtain gauge
* Yarn needle

FINISHED MEASUREMENTS

8 inches in circumference, 11 inches long

GAUGE

14 half double crochets/12 rows = 4 inches

PATTERN

Start making the upper hand

* With Color A, chain 26. Slip stitch in the first chain to form a ring.
* Round 1: Chain 2, work 32 half double crochets into the center of the ring, slip stitch in the first half double crochet to join the round—32 half double crochets total.
* Round 2: Chain 2, half double crochet in each stitch around. Changing to Color B, slip stitch in the first half double crochet to join the round.
* Rounds 3–4: With Color B, work as for Round 2, changing to Color A at the end of Round 4.
* Round 5: With Color A, work as for Round 2.

Make the thumb

* Round 1: Continuing with Color A, chain 1, slip stitch in each of the next 4 stitches, chain 12 for the thumbhole, slip stitch in the chain-1 at the beginning of the round to join.
* Round 2: Chain 2, work 1 half double crochet in each of the 12 chains and in each of the 4 slip stitches around the thumbhole, slip stitch in the first half double crochet to join—16 half double crochets total.
* Round 3: Chain 2, half double crochet in each of the first 2 stitches, decrease over the next 2 stitches (see page 68), *half double crochet in each of the next 2 stitches, decrease over the next 2 stitches*. Repeat from * to * 2 more times, slip stitch in the first stitch to join the round—12 half double crochets total. Fasten off.
* On the following rounds, you'll continue to work across the palm. You'll be working some decreases on both sides of the thumb and at the opposite edge of the palm to make a hand shape.

more

Half Double Crochet Decrease

To make a half double crochet decrease: Yarn over, insert your hook into the next stitch, draw up a loop, yarn over, insert your hook into the next stitch, draw up a loop, yarn over, draw the yarn through all 5 loops on your hook.

Make the lower hand and arm

* Round 1: With Color B and beginning in the right corner stitch of the thumb, join the yarn and chain 2. Working into the remaining loop of each foundation chain of the thumb, half double crochet in each chain around for a total of 14 half double crochets. Working into the remaining stitches from the upper hand, half double crochet in each stitch around for a total of 30 half double crochets. Slip stitch in the first half double crochet from the beginning of the round to join the round—44 half double crochets total.

* Round 2: With Color A, chain 2, half double crochet in each stitch around, slip stitch in the first half double crochet to join the round.

* Round 3: Chain 2, decrease over the first 2 stitches, half double crochet in each of the next 11 stitches, decrease over the next 2 stitches, half double crochet in each of the next 29 stitches. Changing to Color B, slip stitch in the first stitch to join—42 half double crochets total.

* Round 4: With Color B, chain 2, decrease over the first 2 stitches, half double crochet in each of the next 9 stitches, *[decrease over the next 2 stitches] twice, half double crochet in each of the next 11 stitches*. Repeat from * to * once. Half double crochet in the last stitch. Changing to Color A, slip stitch in the first stitch to join the round—37 half double crochets total.

* Round 5: With Color A, chain 2, decrease over the first 2 stitches, half double crochet in each of the next 7 stitches, *[decrease over the next 2 stitches] twice, half double crochet in each of the next 9 stitches*. Repeat from * to * once. Decrease over the last 2 stitches. Changing to Color B, slip stitch in the first stitch to join the round—31 half double crochets total.

* Round 6: With Color B, chain 2, decrease over the first 2 stitches, half double crochet in each of the next 3 stitches, [decrease over the next 2 stitches] twice, half double crochet in each of the next 20 stitches, decrease over the next 2 stitches. Changing to Color A, slip stitch in the first stitch to join the round—27 half double crochets total.

* Round 7: With Color A, chain 2, decrease over the first 2 stitches, half double crochet in the next stitch, [decrease over the next 2 stitches] twice, half double crochet in each of the next 18 stitches, decrease over the next 2 stitches. Slip stitch in the first stitch to join the round—23 half double crochets total.

* Continue without shaping for 8 more rounds as follows.

* Round 8: Chain 2, half double crochet in each stitch around, slip stitch in the first half double crochet to join the round.

* To fit nicely, the mitt now needs just a bit of increasing around the bottom edge. If you want to add any length to the mitt, do so after this shaping.

* Round 9–10: With Color B, chain 2, half double crochet in each of the first 4 stitches, 2 half double crochets in the next stitch, *half double crochet in each of the next 4 stitches, 2 half double crochets in the next stitch*. Repeat from * to * 2 more times. Half double crochet in each of the last 3 stitches. Changing to Color A, slip stitch in the first half double crochet to join the round—27 half double crochets total.

* Rounds 11–16: Repeat Round 9, working in the following color sequence: 1 round each with Color A and then Color B, 2 rounds with Color A, and 2 rounds with Color B, changing to Color A in the last stitch of Round 16.

* Round 17: With Color A, chain 2, half double crochet in each stitch around. Changing to Color B, slip stitch in the first half double crochet to join the round.

* Round 18: With Color B, work as for Round 17.

* Rounds 19–20: With Color A, work as for Round 17.

* Fasten off and weave in the yarn ends.

Juliet Vest

Pattern by Amy O'Neill Houck

SKILLS Chain, single crochet, half double crochet, working in the back loop only, weaving in ends, seaming

This romantic layering piece is the perfect thing to wear while flirting with your favorite Romeo. The vest is actually made entirely of rectangles. You make two identical panels and then crochet them together at the center of the back and at the underarms before adding an edging and border.

MATERIALS

* Brown Sheep Lamb's Pride Worsted yarn (85% wool, 15% mohair; 190 yds/173m per 4 oz/113g) 2 (3, 3, 4) skeins in Brite Blue #M57 [Color A]
* 1 ball Noro Kureyon yarn (100% wool; 110 yds/100m per 1.7 oz/50g) in color #150 [Color B]
* Substitution: Approximately 400 (475, 550, 650) yds/366 (434, 503, 594) m in Color A and 50 yds/46m in Color B of worsted weight wool
* 6mm (size J) hook, or size needed to obtain gauge
* Stitch marker
* Yarn needle
* Tape measure

SIZES

XS (S, M, L)

These sizes correspond to the following chest measurements: 34 (35, 36, 38) inches

GAUGE

14 half double crochets/ 10 rows = 4 inches

PATTERN

Make the vest half (Make 2)

Start the front panel

* With Color A, chain 34 (35, 36, 37).
* Row 1: Half double crochet in the third chain from your hook and in each chain across—32 (33, 34, 35) half double crochets total. Turn.
* Row 2: Chain 2. Half double crochet in the *back loop only* (see page 29) of the first stitch, and in the *back loop only* of each stitch across the row (do not work a stitch in the turning chain)—32 (33, 34, 35) half double crochets total. Turn.
* Repeat Row 2 until your work measures 2½ (2¾, 3, 3½) inches from the foundation chain.

Start the shoulder panel

* At the end of the next row, chain 82, insert a stitch marker in the last stitch. Turn.
* Row 1: Half double crochet in the third chain from your hook and in each chain across the row. Continue to work a half double crochet in the *back loop only* of each stitch across the previous row (do not work a stitch in the turning chain)—112 (113, 114, 115) half double crochets total. Turn.
* Row 2: Chain 2. Half double crochet in the *back loop only* of each stitch across. Turn.
* Repeat Row 2 until the shoulder panel measures 4 (4¼, 4½, 5) inches not including the width of the front panel where they're connected.
* Fasten off.

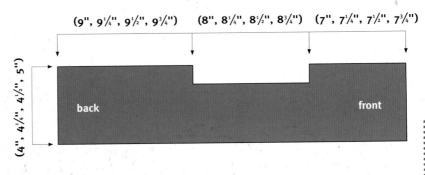

(9", 9¼", 9½", 9¾")   (8", 8¼", 8½", 8¾")   (7", 7¼", 7½", 7¾")

(4", 4¼", 4½", 5")

back   front

more

Size It Up

When a pattern includes multiple sizes, like this one does, the smallest size is always listed first. Then the others are put in parentheses, separated by commas, like this: XS (S, M, L). Instructions for each size are then listed in exactly that way throughout the pattern. To avoid getting confused, it's a good idea to go through the pattern before starting and highlight only the instructions for your size.

Most patterns for tops—such as vests, shrugs, and sweaters—list the chest, or bust, measurement in the sizing section. You should make the size that's the closest to your own chest measurement. How do you know what your measurement is? Grab a trusted friend or family member to help and go like this:

Have your friend wrap a tape measure around the fullest part of your bust, without squeezing. (That's why it's good to have someone help; it's hard to hold that tape measure in place without squeezing when you do it by yourself.) That's your chest circumference. Write down the number so you have it for reference. You'll find chest measurements in the Juliet Vest (page 70) and the Honor Roll Vest (page 90).

To find out more about standard clothing and accessories measurements, check out the Craft Yarn Council of America's website at www.yarnstandards.com.

Start the back panel

* Join the yarn in the stitch marked with the stitch marker. Working along the shoulder panel toward the front panel, work a half double crochet in the *remaining loop* of the chain in each of the first 53 (54, 55, 56) stitches. Chain 2, turn.

* Row 1: Half double crochet in the *back loop only* of the first stitch, and in the *back loop only* of each stitch across the row (do not work a stitch in the turning chain)—53 (54, 55, 56) half double crochets total.

Which Side Are You On?

In crochet we refer to fabric as having a *right side* and a *wrong side*. The right side is the side that will be facing out when the project is completed—the side that everyone sees. The wrong side is the side that isn't shown, like the inside of a bag or the side of a garment that lays against your skin.

* Row 2: Chain 2. Half double crochet in the *back loop only* of each stitch across the row. Turn.

* Repeat Row 2 until the back panel measures 2½ (2¾, 3, 3½) inches.

* Fasten off.

FINISHING

Assemble the vest

1. Lay the two halves of the vest on top of each other with the right sides together and the front and back panels matching.

2. Slip stitch the center back seam.

3. To make the side seams, unfold the garment so it lays open. The seam should be on the wrong side. Fold the vest in half so the bottom edge of the front and back are touching, right sides together. Slip stitch from the bottom edge up on each side, joining the front to the back with an 8- (8-, 7¾-, 7½-) inch seam for the side seams, leaving the rest free for the armholes.

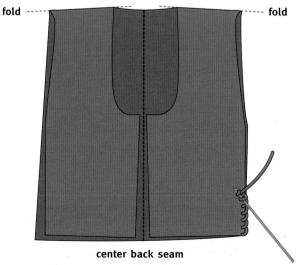

center back seam

Add the edging

* Using Color B, join the yarn at the bottom edge of the front panel. Single crochet up the vest front, around the neckline, and down the other edge. Chain 1, turn.

* Add the eyelet border on the front:

* Continuing where you left off, *single crochet in each of the next 3 stitches, chain 1. Skip 1 single crochet, single crochet in each of the next 3 stitches*. Repeat from * to * across the front vest edge. (At the end of the row, you may end with fewer than 3 single crochets.) Do not continue around the neckline. Chain 1, turn.

* Single crochet in each single crochet and chain of the row. Fasten off and weave in the yarn ends.

* Repeat for the second side of the vest.

Make the tie

* Using Color A, chain 130 (134, 138, 142). Lace the tie through the eyelets to check the length, adjusting the length of the chain if you like.

* Fasten off and weave in the yarn ends.

Camo Bag

Pattern by Julie Armstrong Holetz

SKILLS Chain, slip stitch, single crochet, half double crochet, decreasing, attaching new yarn, weaving in ends, seaming

This bag is easy to make—it's crocheted in the round—and oh-so-trendy. We made it in pink and camouflage, but feel free to change the color and go for something bold or classic. Whatever you like!

MATERIALS

* 1 skein Red Heart Super Saver Multicolor yarn (100% acrylic; 260 yds/238m per 5 oz/141g) in Camouflage #971 [Color A]
* Elmore-Pisgah Peaches & Créme yarn (100% cotton; 122 yds/112m per 2.5 oz/71g): 1 ball each in Shocking Pink #31 [Color B], Peacock #19 [Color C], White #1 [Color D], and Sunburst #11 [Color E]
* Substitution: Approximately 250 yds/110m in Color A and 75 yds/68m in each contrasting color of worsted weight yarn
* 4.5mm (size G) hook, or size needed to obtain gauge
* Stitch markers
* Yarn needle
* Two 1⅝-inch (40mm) plastic O or D rings (available at most crafts stores)
* Tape measure or ruler
* ½ yd (46 cm) of 44-inch- (112cm-) wide cotton or cotton blend fabric
* Scissors
* Straight pins or safety pins
* Sewing needle and thread to match fabric
* Iron
* Ironing board
* 1 adhesive-backed Velcro square

FINISHED MEASUREMENTS

14 inches wide x 9 inches high, not including strap

GAUGE

14 half double crochets/11 rows = 4 inches

PATTERN

Make the body

* With Color A, chain 97. Slip stitch in the first chain to form a ring, taking care not to twist the chain.
* Round 1: Half double crochet in the second chain and in each chain around. Slip stitch in the first half double crochet to join the round—96 half double crochets total.
* Round 2: Chain 1. Half double crochet in the first stitch and in each stitch around. Slip stitch in the first half double crochet to join the round.
* Rounds 3–18: Repeat Round 2. Fasten off.
* Round 19: Attach Color C, chain 1. Half double crochet in each of the first 2 stitches, half double crochet decrease (see page 68) over the next 2 stitches, *half double crochet in each of the next 14 stitches, half double crochet decrease over the next 2 stitches*. Repeat from * to * 4 more times. Half double crochet in each of the last 12 stitches. Slip stitch in the first half double crochet to join the round—90 half double crochets total. Fasten off.
* Round 20: Attach Color A, repeat Round 2. Fasten off.
* Round 21: Attach Color D, chain 1. Single crochet in each of the first 3 stitches, single crochet decrease over the next 2 stitches, *single crochet in each of the next 13 stitches, single crochet decrease over the next 2 stitches*. Repeat from * to * 4 more times. Single crochet in each of last 10 stitches. Slip stitch in the first single crochet to join the round—84 single crochets total. Fasten off.
* Round 22: Attach Color B, repeat Round 2. Fasten off.

more ❧

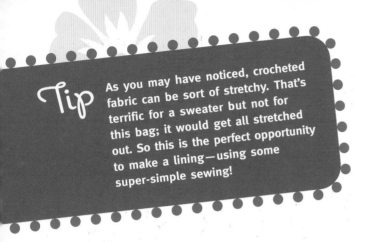

Tip As you may have noticed, crocheted fabric can be sort of stretchy. That's terrific for a sweater but not for this bag; it would get all stretched out. So this is the perfect opportunity to make a lining—using some super-simple sewing!

* Round 23: Attach Color A, chain 1. Single crochet in each of the first 4 stitches, single crochet decrease over the next 2 stitches, *single crochet in each of the next 12 stitches, single crochet decrease over the next 2 stitches*. Repeat from * to * 4 more times. Single crochet in each of the last 8 stitches. Slip stitch in the first single crochet to join the round—78 single crochets total. Fasten off.

* Round 24: Attach Color E, chain 1. Single crochet in the first stitch and in each stitch around. Slip stitch in the first single crochet to join. Fasten off.

* Round 25: Attach Color B, chain 1. Single crochet in each of the first 3 stitches, place a stitch marker, single crochet in each of the next 39 stitches, place a second stitch marker, single crochet in each of the next 36 stitches. Slip stitch in the first single crochet to join the round.

* Fasten off and weave in the yarn ends.

Make the ring tabs

* Row 1: With the right side facing, attach Color B at either one of the stitch markers, chain 1. Single crochet in the same stitch where you joined the yarn and in each of the next 5 stitches—6 single crochets total. Turn.

* Rows 2–7: Chain 1. Single crochet in each stitch across the row. Turn.

* Row 8: Chain 1. Single crochet in each stitch across the row. Fasten off, leaving an 8-inch yarn tail.

* For the second ring tab, repeat Rows 1–8 at the second marker.

Make the strap

* With Color B and leaving a 12-inch yarn tail before the slip knot, chain 114. Turn.

* Row 1: Single crochet in the second chain and in each chain across—113 single crochets total. Fasten off. Turn.

* Row 2: Attach Color E, chain 1. Single crochet in the first stitch and in each stitch across. Fasten off. Turn.

* Row 3: Attach Color A, repeat Row 2.

* Row 4: Attach Color B, chain 1. Half double crochet in the first stitch and in each stitch across. Fasten off. Turn.

* Row 5: Attach Color D, repeat Row 2.

* Row 6: Attach Color C, chain 1. Single crochet in the first stitch and in each stitch across. Fasten off.

FINISHING

Seam the bottom

* Turn the bag inside out. Attach Color A in a corner stitch and, using the yarn needle, slip stitch the foundation edge together to seam. Fasten off.

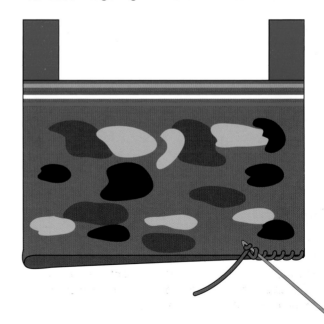

Attach the O-rings and strap

1. Fold one tab over one ring. Thread the yarn needle with the remaining yarn tail and whip stitch (see page 44) the tab to the last row of the bag body. Fasten off and weave in the yarn ends. Repeat for the second tab and ring.

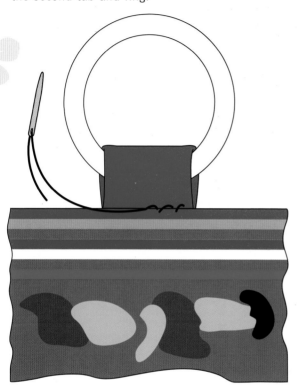

2. Thread the short ends of the strap through both rings from the inside out. Taking care not to twist the strap, bring the short ends together and slip stitch the edges, through both thicknesses, to seam. Adjust the strap so that the seam is hidden in the layer underneath.

Create the lining

1. Using the tape measure, measure your finished bag and cut a piece of cotton fabric that is ½ inch wider than the bag (to allow for the two ¼-inch seams) and twice the length plus ½ inch longer than the bag (to allow for the folded edge). If your bag measures 9 x 14 inches, you will need a piece of fabric that is 18½ x 14½ inches.

2. Fold the piece of fabric in half lengthwise and pin the sides together. Using the sewing needle and thread, stitch the side seams with a running stitch. Fold down the fabric ¼ inch along the top edge and press the seam using an iron.

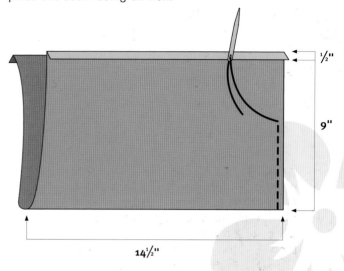

3. Insert the lining into the bag and pin the top edge to the inside of the bag along the second row of crochet stitches from the top. Using the sewing needle and thread, sew the lining to the bag securely. Tack the bottom corners of the lining to the body of the bag with little stitches to keep the lining in place.

4. To add a closure, attach an adhesive-backed Velcro square in the center of the top edge of the lining. For more stability, stitch around each piece of Velcro with the sewing needle and the thread.

Flower Power Pillow

Pattern by Michelle Grissam

SKILLS Chain, slip stitch, single crochet, half double crochet, double crochet, working in the front loop only, weaving in ends, seaming

Express your individuality by making this flower pillow in any colors you like! See a view of another color combination on page 7. You can even play with the placement of the flower so the pillow totally reflects your own taste. The pillowcase is crocheted all in one piece in the round. You then crochet the flower separately and sew it on. Fun!

MATERIALS

* Caron Simply Soft Brites yarn (100% acrylic; 330 yds/302m per 6 oz/170g): 2 skeins in Watermelon #9604 [Color A]; 1 skein each in Mango #9605 [Color B] and Lemonade #9606 [Color C]. The version on page 7 uses 2 skeins Black and 1 skein each of White and Red.
* Substitution: 660 yds/604m of Color A, 100 yds/91m total of Colors B and C in worsted weight yarn
* 5.5mm (size I/9) hook or size need to obtain gauge
* 14-inch-square pillow form
* Yarn needle

FINISHED MEASUREMENTS

14 x 14-inch square tube

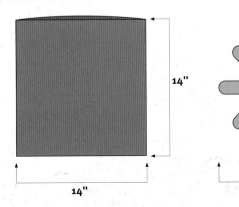

14"

14"

10"

GAUGE

13 crossed bar stitches = 6 inches

5 rows = 2 inches

PATTERN

Make the pillow cover

* With Color A, chain 52.
* Round 1: Working in the *front loop only:* single crochet in the second chain from your hook, chain 1, skip 1 chain, *single crochet in the next chain, chain 1, skip 1 chain*. Repeat from * to * until 1 chain remains. Work [single crochet, chain 1, single crochet] in the last chain, chain 1. Working across the opposite side of your foundation chain in the *unworked back loop only:* skip the next chain. Repeat from * to * until 1 chain remains (this is the chain that you made your very first single crochet in), single crochet in the last chain, chain 1. Slip stitch in the first single crochet to join—52 single crochets total.
* Round 2: Slip stitch into the first chain-1 space, chain 1, *work crossed bar stitch (see page 80), chain 1*. Repeat from * to * 24 more times. Work crossed bar stitch increase, chain 1. Continuing around, work 26 crossed bar stitches. Work 1 crossed bar stitch increase in the next chain-1 space (see page 81), chain 1. Work 1 crossed bar stitch, ending in the same space as the first crossed bar stitch, chain 1. Slip stitch in the beginning chain-1 space to join—54 crossed bar stitches total.

Tip When a pattern calls for a
particular combination of
stitches to be made repeatedly,
the directions for the stitches
will be explained separately in
the beginning of the pattern so
it doesn't have to be repeated
over and over each time it
appears in the instructions.

Special Stitches

Crossed Bar Stitch: Yarn over, insert your hook in the same chain-1 space, yarn over and draw up a loop, yarn over, insert your hook in the next chain-1 space, yarn over and draw up a loop, yarn over, draw the yarn through all 5 loops on your hook.

Crossed Bar Stitch Increase: [Yarn over, insert your hook in the same chain-1 space, yarn over and draw up a loop] twice, yarn over and draw the yarn through all 5 loops on your hook.

Crossed Bar Stitch Decrease: [Yarn over, insert your hook in the next chain-1 space, yarn over and draw up a loop] twice, yarn over and draw the yarn through all 5 loops on your hook.

* Round 3: Chain 1, beginning in the same chain-1 space as the joining slip stitch, work [crossed bar stitch, chain 1] 25 times. Work 1 crossed bar stitch increase, chain 1. Work 1 crossed bar stitch, chain 1. Work 1 crossed bar stitch increase, chain 1. Work [crossed bar stitch, chain 1] 26 times. Work [crossed bar stitch increase in the same space, chain 1. Work crossed bar stitch, chain 1] 2 times. Join with a slip stitch in the first chain-1 space—58 crossed bar stitches total.

* Round 4: Chain 1, beginning in the same chain-1 space as the joining slip stitch, work [crossed bar stitch, chain 1] all the way around the ring. Join with a slip stitch in the first chain-1 space—58 crossed bar stitches total.

* Rounds 5–34: Repeat Round 4. You are forming a tube and will place your pillow form inside. The side facing you is the right side (see page 72 for more on right and wrong sides of your work).

* After Round 34 is finished, insert the pillow form. You will now start decreasing to narrow the top of the pillow cover.

* Round 35: Chain 1, work [crossed bar stitch, chain 1] 21 times. Work [(crossed bar stitch decrease, chain 1] 2 times. Work [crossed bar stitch, chain 1] 25 times. Work [crossed bar stitch decrease, chain 1] 2 times. Work [crossed bar stitch, chain 1] 4 times. Join with a slip stitch in the first chain-1 space—54 crossed bar stitches total.

* Round 36: Chain 1, work [crossed bar stitch, chain 1] 21 times. Work crossed bar stitch decrease, chain 1. Work [crossed bar stitch, chain 1] 25 times. Work crossed bar stitch decrease, chain 1. Work [crossed bar stitch, chain 1] 4 times. Join with a slip stitch in the first chain-1 space—52 crossed bar stitches total.

* Round 37: Chain 1, work [crossed bar stitch, chain 1] around the ring. Join with a slip stitch to the first chain-1 space.

* Round 38: Chain 1, single crochet in the same chain-1 space as the joining slip stitch, chain 1, [single crochet in the next chain-1 space, chain 1] 19 times, single crochet in each of the next 3 chain-1 spaces, chain 1, [single crochet in the next chain-1 space, chain 1] 23 times, single crochet in each of the next 3 chain-1 spaces, chain 1, [single crochet in the next chain-1 space, chain 1] 3 times. Join with a slip stitch in the first single crochet—52 single crochets total.

* Round 39: Chain 1, single crochet in the same single crochet as the joining slip stitch, single crochet in the next chain-1 space, [single crochet in the next single crochet, single crochet in the next chain-1 space] 19 times. [Insert your hook in the next single crochet, yarn over and draw up a loop] 3 times, yarn over and draw the yarn through all 4 loops on your hook. Single crochet in the next chain-1 space, [single crochet in the next single crochet, single crochet in the next chain-1 space] 23 times. [Insert your hook in the next single crochet, yarn over and draw up a loop] 3 times, yarn over and draw the yarn through all 4 loops on your hook. Single crochet in the next chain-1 space, [single crochet in the next single crochet, single crochet in the next chain-1 space] 3 times. Join with a slip stitch to the first single crochet—96 single crochets total.

* Fasten off, leaving a 30-inch yarn tail. Insert the pillow form. Thread the yarn needle with the yarn tail, line up the stitches along the top of the pillow cover, and whip stitch (see page 44) the opening closed.

Make the center of the flower

* With Color C, chain 4. Join with a slip stitch in the first chain to form a ring.

* Round 1: Chain 3 (counts as first double crochet), work 11 double crochets into the ring. Slip stitch in the third chain of the beginning chain-3 to join the round—12 double crochets total.

* Round 2: Chain 3 (counts as the first double crochet), double crochet in the same stitch as the beginning chain-3. Work 2 double crochets in each stitch around. Slip stitch in the third chain of the beginning chain-3 to join the round—24 double crochets total.

* Fasten off and weave in the yarn ends.

Make the flower petals

* With Color B, join the yarn with a slip stitch in any stitch of the flower center.

* Round 1: *Chain 17. Half double crochet in the third chain from your hook (counts as a chain-2 space) and in each chain around the ring. Slip stitch in each of the next 3 double crochets of the flower center*. Repeat from * to * around. Slip stitch in the first slip stitch to join the round—8 petals total.

* Round 2: Chain 1. Working in the stitches on each side of the petals: *single crochet in the next chain stitch and in each chain stitch around. Work 2 single crochets in the chain-2 space at the end of the petal, single crochet in each half double crochet around. Working over the slip stitch and into the double crochet from Round 2 of the flower center, [insert your hook in the next double crochet, yarn over and draw up a loop] 3 times, yarn over and draw the yarn through all 4 loops on your hook*. Repeat from * to * 7 more times. Join with a slip stitch in the first single crochet.

* Round 3: Chain 1, single crochet in the same single crochet as joining slip stitch, single crochet in each of the next 14 single crochets, [work 2 single crochets in the next single crochet] twice. *Single crochet in each of the next 31 single crochets around the petal, [work 2 single crochets in the next single crochet] 2 times*. Repeat from * to * 6 more times. Single crochet in each of the next 16 single crochets. Join with a slip stitch to the first single crochet.

* Fasten off, leaving a very long yarn tail for sewing the flower to the top of the pillow. Weave in the yarn ends.

* Thread the yarn needle with the yarn tail and sew the flower to the pillow cover with a running stitch. Fasten off and weave in the yarn end.

A chain-1 space

A chain-1 space is the small hole underneath the spot where you made a chain and skipped a stitch in the previous row. When a pattern says to work a stitch or stitches into a chain-1 (or chain-2, chain-3, etc.) space, simply work those stitches as usual by inserting your hook into the hole and making the stitches around the chain.

Ruby Slippers

Pattern by Vashti Braha

SKILLS Chain, slip stitch, single crochet, increasing, decreasing, working in the front loop only, working in the back loop only, joining new yarn, weaving in ends, seaming

These glittery slippers are worked flat in rows of single crochet. Then, when you wave your yarn needle wand along the seams, they magically become ballet slippers. And just think: If you can make ruby slippers, then you can make emerald, sapphire, and diamond slippers, too!

MATERIALS

* 1 skein Lion Brand Wool-Ease Chunky yarn (80% acrylic, 20% wool; 153 yds/140m per 5 oz/140g) in Red #112
* Substitution: Approximately 153 yds/140m of chunky weight yarn, in wool, acrylic, or wool blend
* 5.5mm (size I) hook, or size needed to obtain gauge
* 2 stitch markers
* Yarn needle
* Red acrylic jewels (optional)
* Fabric glue (such as Aleene's Platinum Bond Fabric Adhesive)
* 24 inches of ⅜-inch-wide ribbon, cut in half (optional)

FINISHED SIZE

Fit women's sock size 8–9 (Medium). Changes for sock sizes 6–7 (Small) and 10–11 (Large) are in italics.

sides

sole

GAUGE

12 single crochets/2 rows = 4 inches

PATTERN

The slipper sole (Make 2)

* Chain 3.
* Row 1: Skip 1 chain, work 2 single crochets in each of the next two chains—4 single crochets total. Turn.
* Row 2: Chain 1. Single crochet in each stitch across the row. Turn.
* Row 3: Chain 1. Work 2 single crochets in the first stitch, single crochet in each of the next 2 stitches, 2 single crochets in the last stitch—6 single crochets total. Turn.
* Rows 4–11: Repeat Row 2. *For size Small,* skip Row 11 and move on to Row 12. *For size Large,* repeat Row 2 once more before moving on to Row 12.
* Row 12: Chain 1. Single crochet in each stitch across to the last stitch, work 2 single crochets in the last stitch—7 single crochets total. Turn.
* Row 13–18: Alternate working Rows 2 and 12. At the end of Row 18 you will have 10 single crochets total.
* Rows 19–25: Chain 1. Single crochet in each stitch across the row. Turn. *For size Large,* repeat Row 2 once more before continuing with Row 26.
* Row 26: Chain 1. Single crochet in each stitch across to the last 2 stitches, work 1 single crochet decrease (see page 43) over the last 2 stitches—9 single crochets total. Turn.
* Row 27–30: Repeat Row 26. At the end of Row 30 you will have 5 single crochets total.
* Place a stitch marker in the first and last stitch of the last row.

more

Begin the toe

Continue where you left off.

* Row 1: Chain 1. Single crochet in the first stitch, *2 single crochets in the next stitch, single crochet in the next stitch*. Repeat from * to * across the row—7 single crochets total. Turn.

* Row 2: Repeat Row 1—10 single crochets total.

* Row 3: Chain 1. Single crochet in the first stitch, 2 single crochets in the next stitch, *single crochet in the next stitch, 2 single crochets in the next stitch*. Repeat from * to * across—15 single crochets total. Turn.

* Rows 4–6: Chain 1. Single crochet in each stitch across the row. Turn.

Begin first side of slipper top

Continue where you left off.

* Row 1: Chain 1. Single crochet in each of the next 5 stitches—5 single crochets total. Turn, leaving the remaining stitches unworked.

* Row 2: Chain 1. Single crochet in each stitch across the row. Turn.

* Row 3: Chain 1. Single crochet in each stitch across to the last 2 stitches; work a single crochet decrease over the last 2 stitches—4 single crochets total.

* Rows 4–20: Chain 1. Single crochet in each stitch across the row. Turn. *For size Small,* skip Row 20 and move on to the heel.

Begin heel of first side

Continue where you left off.

* Row 1: Chain 1. Single crochet in each stitch across to the last stitch, work 2 single crochets in the last stitch—5 single crochets total. Turn.

* Rows 2–6: Chain 1. Single crochet in each stitch across the row. Turn.

* Fasten off.

* Begin second side of slipper top:

* Attach the yarn in the 5th stitch from the end of Row 6 of the toe section.

* Row 1: Chain 1, single crochet in the same stitch and in each of the remaining 4 stitches of the row—5 single crochets total. Turn.

* Row 2: Chain 1. Single crochet in each stitch across the row. Turn.

* Row 3: Chain 1, work a single crochet decrease over the first 2 stitches, single crochet in each remaining stitch across the row—4 single crochets total. Turn.

* Rows 4–20: Chain 1. Single crochet in each stitch across the row. Turn. *For size Small,* skip Row 20 and move on to the heel.

Begin heel of second side

Continue where you left off.

* Row 1: Chain 1, work 2 single crochets in the first stitch, single crochet in each of the remaining 3 stitches—5 single crochets total. Turn.

* Rows 2–6: Chain 1. Single crochet in each stitch across the row. Turn.

* Row 7: Bring the short ends of the heel together and, working through both layers, slip stitch the two sides together—5 slip stitches total. Do not fasten off.

Seam the sole to the sides

1. Fold the slipper along the marked row, bringing the end of the heel to the very first row. Make sure to determine which side is the inside, or wrong side, for each foot so the shaping will fit the foot correctly.

2. Thread the yarn needle with a 48-inch length of the same color yarn (white was used here for clarity) and, working on the wrong side of the slipper, attach the yarn in one of the marked stitches at the toe. Seam the top of the slipper to the sole with a whipstitch, being sure to also sew through the side of the first and last toe stitches to avoid leaving a hole.

3. Continue to sew the top of the slipper to the sole, taking care to line up the rows. When you reach the heel seam, make sure it is centered on the foundation row. Continue seaming the top and sole together around the opposite side, ending at the second stitch marker. Fasten off. Turn the slipper right side out.

Edge the slipper opening for a perfect fit

Before you crochet the trim, try on the slippers for fit. If the slipper opening fits well, work both slip stitch rows below with the same size crochet hook you used to make the slippers. If the opening is too loose, work the slip stitch rows with a slightly smaller hook.

Attach the yarn in any stitch at the top of the heel seam.

* *For size Small:* Work 1 slip stitch in each row end, skipping every fourth row until you get to the 5 single crochet stitches of the toe. Slip stitch in the *back loop only* (see page 29) of each of the 5 toe stitches.

  Continue working 1 slip stitch in each row end, skipping every fourth row, of the second side until you reach the first slip stitch. Do not join.

  Work one more round of slip stitches, working through the back loop only.

* *For sizes Medium and Large:* Work 1 slip stitch in each row end, skipping every third row until you get to the 5 single crochet stitches of the toe. Slip stitch in the *back loop only* of each of the 5 toe stitches.

Continue working 1 slip stitch in each row end, skipping every third row, of the second side until you reach the first slip stitch. Do not join.

Work one more round of slip stitches, working through the *back loop only*.

When you've finished the steps above, try on the slipper again for fit. If the opening is too tight, rework both slip stitch rows with a slightly larger crochet hook. If the opening is too loose, rework the slip stitch rows with a slightly smaller hook. Then fasten off and weave in the yarn ends.

BLOCKING

To block slippers, stuff them with crumpled pieces of paper or plastic bags. Don't stuff too much—just enough so the slippers hold their shape nicely. Lightly spray water on all parts of the slipper using a spray bottle. Let the slippers air-dry fully overnight.

FINISHING

For gem-studded slippers, glue red acrylic jewels to the outside of the slippers with fabric glue and let them air-dry overnight.

There's no place like home when you're wearing ruby slippers!

For slippers with bows, weave one end of a length of ribbon through the *back loops only* of every other slip stitch of 7 stitches at the front center of a slipper. Tie the ends into a bow. Repeat for the other slipper.

Here's another version—skip the jewels and add a cute bow instead.

Peek-a-Boo Shrug

Pattern by Mary Jane Hall

SKILLS Chain, single crochet, double crochet, joining new yarn, working in the back loop only, weaving in ends, seaming

A shrug is just a glorified rectangle—seriously! The slightly lacy body of this shrug is crocheted first, then you seam up the sleeves and add the ribbing after you're done.

MATERIALS

* 1 skein Bernat Super Value yarn (100% acrylic; 382 yds/350m per 7 oz/197g) in Medium Sea Green
* Substitution: Approximately 300 yds/274m of medium worsted weight yarn
* 6mm (size J) hook, or size needed to obtain gauge
* 2 stitch markers
* Straight pins
* Yarn needle

FINISHED MEASUREMENTS

Shrug fits chest measurements: 32 (40) inches

Finished size before seaming: 12 (13) inches wide x 33 inches long

GAUGE

Body: 8 stitches [double crochet, chain 1]/8 rows = 5 inches

Ribbing: 16 stitches [single crochet through the *back loop only*]/ 16 rows = 4 inches

PATTERN

* Chain 106.
* Row 1: Skip the first 4 chains (counts as double crochet and chain 1), *double crochet in the next chain, chain 1, skip 1 chain*. Repeat from * to * across until 2 chains remain. Double crochet in each of the last 2 chains—53 double crochets and 51 chain-1 spaces total. Turn.
* Row 2: Chain 4 (counts as double crochet and chain 1). Skip the first 2 double crochets, *double crochet in the next chain-1 space, chain 1, skip the next double crochet*. Repeat from * to * across the row, ending with double crochet in the last chain-4 space, double crochet in the third chain of the beginning chain-4. Turn.
* Rows 3–18 (20): Repeat Row 2. Fasten off.

(Note: When instructions are included for different sizes, they're given with the smallest size first, followed by the larger sizes in parentheses. So in this case, for the smaller size, repeat Row 2 for Rows 3–18. For the larger size, repeat Row 2 for Rows 3–20.)

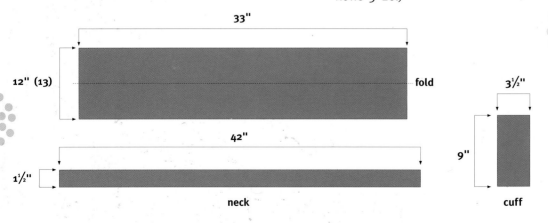

33"

12" (13)   fold

42"

1½"

neck

3½"

9"

cuff

more

Seam the sleeves

* Fold the rectangle in half lengthwise. Place a stitch marker in the 11th double crochet in from each edge. Using the yarn needle and matching yarn, start at one edge of the shrug and whip stitch (see page 44) the edges together up to the stitch marker. Fasten off and repeat for the second sleeve. The opening between the sleeves should measure about 20 inches.

(Note: The opening may seem too large at this point, but adding the ribbed cuff will give the shrug a better fit.)

Add edging to the body opening

* With the right side facing you, attach the yarn with a slip stitch in any stitch along the edge of the body opening. Chain 1, single crochet in the same stitch and in each double crochet and in each chain stitch around the entire edge. You should have about 126 single crochets total.
* Fasten off.

Add edging to the sleeves

* With the right side facing you, attach the yarn with a slip stitch to the bottom edge of a sleeve. Working into the ends of each row, work 27 (30) single crochet evenly around the sleeve edge, alternating 1 single crochet in the end of one row and 2 single crochets in the end of the next row. Repeat for the other sleeve.

Make ribbing for the body

* Chain 7.
* Row 1: Working in the *back loop only,* single crochet in the second chain from your hook and in each chain across the row—6 single crochets total. Turn.
* Row 2: Chain 1. Working in the *back loop only,* single crochet in each stitch across the row. Turn.
* Rows 3–102 (106): Repeat Row 2.
* Fasten off. Fold the ribbing in half and whip stitch the short ends together.

Why not make a Chunky Hat in green to match your new shrug? For directions on making this flowered hat, just log onto www.get-hooked.net.

Make the sleeve cuff (Make 2)

* Chain 13.
* Row 1: Working in the *back loop only,* single crochet in the second chain from your hook and in each chain across the row—12 single crochets total. Turn.
* Row 2: Chain 1. Working in the *back loop only,* single crochet in each stitch across the row. Turn.
* Rows 3–27 (30): Repeat Row 2.
* Fasten off. Fold the cuff in half and whip stitch the short ends together.

FINISHING

Neck edge

* There are 24 (20) fewer rows on the body ribbing than there are stitches around the body opening of the shrug, so place the stitch markers at 24 (20) places evenly spaced around the shrug edge. To do this, fold the shrug in half and place the stitch markers at each half; then place the stitch markers at each quarter. Now place 5 (4) stitch markers evenly spaced in each quarter.

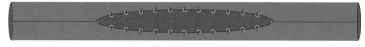

* With right sides together, pin the cuff along the edge of the shrug. Using the yarn needle and matching yarn, whip stitch the cuff to the shrug, skipping each stitch where stitch markers are placed. Fasten off. Remove the stitch markers.

* Attach the sleeve cuff:
* With right sides together, whip stitch the row end of a cuff to each stitch along a sleeve edge. Fasten off. Repeat for the second sleeve. Weave in all yarn ends.

Hot... or Not?

Crochet is so quiet and portable, it's tempting to do it everywhere. But remember, not everyone is a crocheter, and most people like to feel that you're paying attention to them (you know, like when your bff is talking about her crush or when your teacher's going over last night's homework). Be courteous when it comes to your crochet and leave it in your bag unless you ask first. Some teachers might be cool with you stitching away, because they believe you when you say you pay better attention when your hands are busy; but it's totally okay for them to insist that you take notes and make eye contact. The last thing you want to do is offend people because you can't keep your hands off your new hobby!

Hot

* In the lunchroom—just make sure you don't spill stuff on your yarn!
* On the bus, train, or subway
* When you're watching TV
* In the doctor's waiting room
* While talking on the phone
* At the movies, as long as you keep your stitches quiet and your elbows to yourself
* Waiting in line for concert tickets or to vote for class president

Not

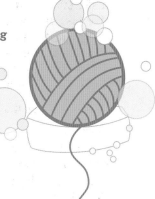

* In class—unless you have the teacher's permission
* During driver's ed.
* When you're watching your baby brother
* In the bath
* At band practice
* At a live performance
* At a party, unless it's a crafty party— people will think you're antisocial!

Honor Roll Vest

Pattern by Annette Petavy

SKILLS Chain, slip stitch, single crochet, double crochet, joining new yarn, working in the back loop only, increasing, decreasing, weaving in ends, seaming

This preppy-with-an-edge vest is sure to get you straight A's in school. The stitch pattern works up fast and the simple increases and decreases create a form-fitting garment.

MATERIALS

* Reynolds Signature yarn (80% acrylic, 20% wool; 220 yds/201m per 100g) 3 (3, 3, 4) skeins in Claret #68
* Substitution: Approximately 550 (660, 660, 770) yds/503 (604, 604, 705) m of worsted weight yarn in wool or wool blend
* 6mm (size J) hook, or size needed to obtain gauge
* Stitch markers
* Yarn needle

FINISHED MEASUREMENTS

Fits chest measurements: 33 (36, 39, 45) inches (Note: This vest looks best layered, so make it about 1 to 2 inches larger than your actual chest measurement.)

GAUGE

Ribbing: 12 stitches [single crochet worked in the *back loop only*]/14 rows = 4 inches, measured *without* stretching

Body: Split-stitch pattern: 8 stitches = 6 inches/ 8 rows = 4 inches

(See page 93 for instructions on how to work your gauge swatch.)

PATTERN

Start with the ribbing for the back

* Chain 13 (13, 13, 15).
* Row 1: Work 1 single crochet into the second chain from your hook and into each remaining chain. Turn.
* Row 2: Chain 1. Work 1 single crochet in the *back loop only* in each stitch from the previous row. Turn.
* Repeat Row 2 for 50 (54, 58, 66) rows. On the right side of your work you have 24 (26, 28, 32) ridges (1 ridge = 2 rows), with one single row at the beginning and at the end. Check the number of ridges, adding or subtracting rows as necessary until you have the correct number.
* Fasten off. Turn the work, right side facing you, so the rib ridges run vertically.

Make the body for the back

* Attach the yarn in the first row of ribbing at the upper right corner of the piece.

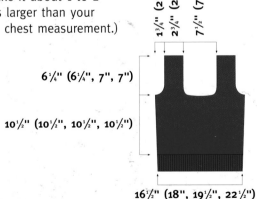

1¾" (2¼", 2¾", 4¼")
2¾" (2¾", 3¼", 3¾")
7½" (7½", 7½", 7½")

6¼" (6¼", 7", 7")

10½" (10½", 10½", 10½")

16½" (18", 19½", 22½")

front

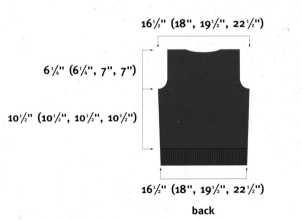

16½" (18", 19½", 22½")

6¼" (6¼", 7", 7")

10½" (10½", 10½", 10½")

16½" (18", 19½", 22½")

back

more

Crochet 101

ch= chain
sc= single crochet
dc= double crochet

don't count
this chain

1
2
3
4

Split-Stitch Pattern

This pattern is composed of 2 double crochets worked in the same space. What makes it different from a regular double crochet increase is that after the first row, each split-stitch is worked into the space *between* the 2 double crochets, forming the split-stitches in the previous row.

Insert your hook between the two double crochets from the previous row.

* Row 1: (Place a stitch marker on the front of this row to mark it as the right side.) Chain 3 (counts as 1 double crochet). Skip the first ridge and make a split-stitch (see page 92) between the first and second ridges. Make a split-stitch in the third ridge. Make a split-stitch in every ridge until 3 ridges remain. Make a split-stitch in the first remaining ridge. Skip the next ridge and make a split-stitch between that ridge and the following one. Work 1 double crochet in the last row of the ribbing. Turn— 22 (24, 26, 30) split-stitches total.

* Row 2: Chain 3 (counts as 1 double crochet). Make a split-stitch in the center of each split-stitch from the previous row. End with 1 double crochet in the third chain of the chain-3 from the previous row. Turn.

* Repeat Row 2 until the work measures 10½ inches, excluding the ribbing; end with a right side row.

Shape the armhole

* Row 1 (with the wrong side facing you): Working into each double crochet stitch, slip stitch in each of the next 3 (5, 5, 9) stitches, single crochet in the next stitch, double crochet in the next stitch. Make a split-stitch in each of the next 18 (18, 20, 20) split-stitches. Double crochet in the next double crochet, single crochet in the next double crochet. Turn.

* Row 2 (with the right side facing you): Slip stitch in each of the next 2 (2, 3, 3) stitches. Chain 3 (counts as 1 double crochet), double crochet in each of the next 0 (0, 1, 1) stitches. Make a split-stitch in each of the next 18 split-stitches. Double crochet in the next 1 (1, 2, 2) stitches.

* Continue working in the split-stitch pattern, working 1 (1, 2, 2) double crochets in the double crochet stitch at each edge, until the work measures 16¾ (16¾, 17½, 17½) inches, excluding the ribbing; end with a right side row.

Shape the shoulders and neck

* Working into each stitch, slip stitch in each of the next 5 (5, 4, 4) stitches, single crochet in the next stitch, double crochet in the next stitch. Make a split-stitch in each of the next 1 (1, 2, 2) split-stitches. Double crochet in the next stitch, single crochet in the next stitch. Slip stitch in each of the next 16 stitches. Single crochet in the next stitch, double crochet in the next stitch. Make a split-stitch in each of the next 1 (1, 2, 2) split-stitches. Double crochet in the next stitch, single crochet in the next stitch, slip stitch in each of the next 5 (5, 4, 4).

* Fasten off and weave in the yarn ends.

Make the front

* Work the ribbing and the body as for the back up to the armhole shaping. For the front, the armhole shaping and neck shaping start on the same row. After this next row, the left side and the right side of the front are worked separately.

Shape the armhole and neck

* With the wrong side facing you, slip stitch in each of the next 3 (5, 5, 9) stitches, single crochet in the next stitch, double crochet in the next stitch. Make a split-stitch in each of the next 5 (5, 6, 6) split-stitches. Double crochet in the next stitch, single crochet in the next stitch. Slip stitch in each of the next 12 stitches. Single crochet in the next stitch, double crochet in the next stitch. Make a split-stitch in each of the next 5 (5, 6, 6) split-stitches. Double crochet in the next stitch, single crochet in the next stitch. Turn.

Shape the left side of the neck

* Row 1: With the right side facing you, slip stitch in each of the next 2 (2, 3, 3) stitches, chain 3 (counts as 1 double crochet), double crochet in each of the next 0 (0, 1, 1) stitches. Make a split-stitch in each

of the next 4 split-stitches. Double crochet in the next stitch, single crochet in the next stitch, slip stitch in the next stitch. Turn.

* Row 2: Skip the slip stitch from the previous row, slip stitch in each of the next 2 stitches. Chain 3 (counts as 1 double crochet), make a split-stitch in each of the next 4 split-stitches. Double crochet in each of the next 1 (1, 2, 2) stitches.

* Continue working in the split-stitch pattern, with 1 double crochet at the neck edge and 1 (1, 2, 2) double crochets at the armhole edge, until the work measures 16¾ (16¾, 17½, 17½) inches, excluding the ribbing; end with a right side row.

Shape the left shoulder

* With the wrong side facing you, chain 3 (counts as 1 double crochet). Make a split-stitch in each of the next 1 (1, 2, 2) split-stitches. Double crochet in the next stitch, single crochet in the next stitch, slip stitch in each of the next 5 (5, 4, 4) stitches.

* Fasten off and weave in the yarn ends.

Shape the right side of the neck

* Row 1: With the right side facing you, join the yarn in the first double crochet of the first split-stitch from the center where you split for the neck shaping. Chain 1, single crochet in the same stitch, double crochet in the next stitch, make a split-stitch in each of the next 4 split-stitches. Double crochet in

each of the next 1(1, 2, 2) stitches. Turn.

* Row 2: Chain 3, double crochet in each of the next 0 (0, 1, 1) stitches. Make a split-stitch in each of the next 4 split-stitches. Double crochet in the next stitch. Turn.

* Continue working in the split-stitch pattern as for the left side of the neck.

Shape the right shoulder

* Slip stitch in each of the next 5 (5, 4, 4) stitches. Single crochet in the next stitch, double crochet in the next stitch. Make a split-stitch in each of the next 1 (1, 2, 2) split-stitches. Double crochet in the next stitch.

* Fasten off and weave in the yarn ends.

FINISHING

Finish the neck

* With the wrong side facing you, attach the yarn in a corner stitch and work one row of single crochet around the neck front as follows. You will sometimes work into the end of a row and sometimes into a stitch: work 2 single crochets into each row, and 1 single crochet into each stitch. Turn.

* Next row: Chain 1. Single crochet in the *back loop only* of each stitch.

* Fasten off and weave in the yarn ends.

* To finish the neck back, repeat as for the front.

Sew the shoulder seams

* With right sides together and using a yarn needle and matching yarn, whip stitch (see page 44) the shoulder seams.

Finish the armholes

* With the wrong side facing you, attach the yarn at the underarm and work one row of single crochet around one of the armholes as follows. You will sometimes work into the end of a row and sometimes into a stitch: work 2 single crochets into each row, and 1 single crochet into each stitch. Turn.

* Next row: Chain 1. Single crochet in the *back loop only* of each stitch.

* Fasten off and weave in the yarn ends.

* Finish the other armhole in the same way.

Sew the side seams

* With right sides together, whip stitch the side seams. Turn the vest right side out.

Gauging Your Vest

Here's how to work your gauge swatch.

* Chain 24.

* Row 1: Work 2 double crochets in the fourth chain from the hook. *Skip 1 chain. Work 2 double crochets in next chain*. Repeat from * to * until 2 chains remain. Skip 1 chain and work 1 double crochet in the last chain.

* Row 2: Chain 3 (this turning chain counts as 1 double crochet). Work 1 split-stitch between each pair of double crochets from the previous row. Finish with 1 double crochet in the top chain of the turning chain from the previous row.

* Repeat Row 2 until your swatch is large enough to measure.

Get More Info

This book is just the beginning! To learn more about yarn and hooks, check out your local library, give crafty people the third degree, and surf the Net for a while—you'll find a huge amount of information about crochet. Your local yarn and crafts stores might offer classes, and your community center is a great place to explore too.

BOOKS & MAGAZINES

There are lots of other crochet books out there, and picking up a magazine is a great way to find trendy patterns and timely information. Take a look at these.

Get Hooked: Simple Steps to Crochet Cool Stuff, by Kim Werker (Watson-Guptill, 2006) is a sister to this book! You'll drool over fifteen awesome patterns!

Teach Yourself VISUALLY Crocheting, by Kim P. Werker and Cecily Keim (Wiley, 2006) has tons of photo-illustrated tutorials for basic and more advanced crochet techniques. I'm biased, though, since I cowrote it!

The Crochet Answer Book, by Edie Eckman (Storey Publishing, 2005) is a tiny handbook that covers all the nitty-gritty crochet stuff you might forget. It's the perfect size to toss into your bag.

The Ultimate Sourcebook of Knitting and Crochet Stitches (Reader's Digest, 2003) is a great collection of stitches—with step-by-step instructions—for you to try!

Check out *Interweave Crochet* for a great view of all that crochet can do.

Knit.1 magazine has tons of crochet too! Check it out quarterly for patterns in the latest fashions and news about what's going on in the world of knitting and crochet.

Crochet Today magazine comes out six times a year and has patterns of all sorts!

WEBSITES

Want to join others who love crochet as much as you do? Find out more at the Crochet Guild of America (CGOA) site: http://www.crochet.org.

For more about yarn weight, hook sizes, and standard body measurements, check out the Craft Yarn Council of America's information at http://www.yarnstandards.com.

Want to find a charity to crochet for? The CGOA has a huge list at http://www.crochet.org/charity2.html.

Want more information or tutorials? Do a simple search for terms such as "crochet tutorials" or "crochet stitches," and you'll find tons of websites to help you out. Also, look up the designers from this book and you'll find some more amazing patterns to make!

YARN COMPANIES

The yarns featured in *Get Hooked Again* are just some of the zillions out there! Take a look at these yarn companies' websites to get a picture of what's available and to find some inspiration:

* Bernat: http://www.bernat.com
* Berroco: http://www.berroco.com/
* Brown Sheep Company, Inc.: http://brownsheep.com/
* Caron: http://caron.com/
* Cascade Yarns: http://cascadeyarns.com/
* Coats & Clark: http://www.coatsandclark.com
* Crystal Palace: http://www.straw.com/cpy
* DMC Thread: http://www.dmc-usa.com
* Elmore Pisgah: http://www.elmore-pisgah.com/
* JCA: http://www.jcacrafts.com
* Lion Brand: http://www.lionbrand.com

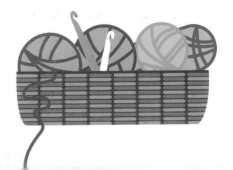

Meet the Designers

Crochet designers from all over contributed the cool patterns in this book. To learn more about them, have some fun on Google!

VASHTI BRAHA (*Ruby Slippers*), a half-Irish girl from the Midwest now living in Florida, serves on the board of directors for the Crochet Guild of America. Her designs have appeared in CGOA's *Pattern Line, Crochet Me, Crochet!,* and *Knit.1,* as well as in books.

MICHELLE GRISSAM (*Flower Power Pillow*) learned how to crochet when she was eleven. She crochets for her children, and they love having something Mommy made for them. Michelle encourages aspiring crocheters to keep working at it!

MARY JANE HALL (*Peek-a-Boo Shrug*) is the owner of Mary Jane's Crochet, which specializes in trendy wearables. She has had designs published in books, magazines, and in booklets called *CROCHET Young and Trendy* and *CROCHET in Style.* Her most recent book was published in fall 2007.

JULIE ARMSTRONG HOLETZ (*Camo Bag*) is the founder of SkaMama Designs, a company dedicated to encouraging kids of all ages to play with crochet. When her own two children allow her some time, Julie is a freelance technical editor and crochet pattern designer. Her very first book, *Crochet Away!,* was published in fall 2006.

AMY O'NEILL HOUCK (*Juliet Vest*) learned to crochet at age eight from her grandmother. She has taught crochet and knitting in libraries, yarn shops, and trains, and publishes patterns online, in books and magazines, and with yarn companies. Amy maintains a fiber blog called The Hook and I.

LAUREN IRVING (*Hook Roll, Crochet-Anywhere Tote*), the owner of Little River Fiber Arts, is addicted to crochet and can often be found sneaking yarn and hooks into inappropriate places.

CHLOE NIGHTINGALE (*Gidget Bucket Hat*) is short and crabby, writes electronic music, and crochets. She just moved to Glasgow, Scotland, and is having a blast!

DORA OHRENSTEIN (*Lacy Choker*) has had numerous crochet fashion designs published in books and magazines. A professional singer and Manhattanite, she adapts New York chic for the hook.

ANNETTE PETAVY (*Honor Roll Vest*) has taken a break from her serious work as a translator to see where her playful crochet hook will lead her. She lives in Alsace, France, with her husband and children.

AMY SWENSON (*Fingerless Street Mitts*) lives a yarn-filled life in Calgary, Canada. She designs under the label "indiKnits" and owns and operates Make One Yarn Studio, a community-based yarn shop. Her first book, *Not Your Mama's Crochet,* was published in fall 2006.

KIM PIPER WERKER (*Autumn Striped Scarf, Chunky Hat, Shelter-Your-Shades Case, Workin'-for-You Scarf*) is the editor of *Interweave Crochet* magazine and is the founder and creative director of the *Crochet Me* online community. Kim has written four books including *Crochet Me,* and *Teach Yourself Visually Crocheting* (co-authored with Cecily Keim). She crochets scarves out of beautiful yarns, makes dolls with quirky personalities, and, when not crocheting, she likes to knit, spin, read good books, and tinker with web sites. Originally from New York State, Kim lives in Vancouver, Canada with her husband and their dog.

Index